TALLY HO THE FOX!

The Foundation for Building World-Visionary, World-Impacting, Reproducing Disciples

Herb Hodges

Hodges, Herb, Author
Tallyho, the Fox / Written by Herb Hodges

ISBN 10: 1-891986-04-X (paperback; softcover)
ISBN 13: 978-1-891986-04-8 (paperback; softcover)

Second Edition.

Unless otherwise noted, the Bible version used in this publication is the KING JAMES VERSION.

Published by Manhattan Source, Incorporated.

Printed in the United States of America.

Introduction

The typical Christian church in America has a giant undeveloped "labor pool" in its membership. The typical Christian is unemployed as far as Christ's standard of employment is concerned, and the typical employed Christian is often "under-employed," spending much time and effort in activities that show very little result in reaching and building people. The typical Christian church meets Sunday by Sunday in an "auditorium" and its members are individual "auditors" forming part of a listening "audience." In short, the typical church is jammed with "pew potatoes" whose only intent is to come to church, listen to a sermon, and go away, hoping that this course will help to privately smuggle their souls to heaven and help them to have a reasonably comfortable life on the way. Any resemblance between this lifestyle and the Christian life pictured in the New Testament is purely coincidental.

It is evident to me that we Christians must re-study the New Testament, our manual of operation, and we must force ourselves to be ruthlessly objective as we do. We must declare ourselves independent of tradition and find out what the New Testament tells us about ourselves and our God-given assignment.

Charles Swindoll wrote, "No group in history has proven itself more effective than that first-century evangelistic team, the inner core of Christ's men." This assessment is unquestionably true, but why? Surely the training process Jesus employed with them is a large factor. This training process revolves around the gigantic word "disciple." That word runs riot through the first five books of the New Testament, occurring 269 times (The Gospel of Matthew through the Book of Acts). It is used both as a noun and as a verb. In addition, the verb form of this word constitutes the only command in the Great Commission which Jesus gave to His followers. "Turn people into disciples," He commanded. In light of the vast multitudes of undeveloped believers in today's church (and many of them in church every time it gathers), can we continue to take it for granted that we have properly interpreted the word 'disciple?' Or, that we have adequately understood the meaning (or the process) of "turning people into disciples?" In light of the poor impact of the church at large, in light of the billions of unevangelized people on earth today, can we continue to believe that we are operating by the Great Commission? I think not.

These pages are a very brief and very poor re-examination and re-interpretation of our identity as believers in Christ and our assignment as His followers. It is my prayer that God will disturb and arouse us through these pages to new perception, new participation, and new productivity in fulfilling the Great Commission of our Lord.

I am indebted to a large number of friends and to a countless number of authors, both "secular" and "sacred," for the vast reservoir of ideas and strategies which have been condensed into these "short-hand" ideas. Also, to many who have encouraged me to "get these things in print" and to a few who have assisted me in doing so. I defer their influence to the Judgment Seat of Christ, which will afford them a better evaluation and a better reward than I can give.

Herb Hodges

Acknowledgements

It is impossible to even be born as a human being without heavy indebtedness. Every human being already owes for nine months of room and board when he is born!

Of all people in heavy debt, I feel like the one with the heaviest debt, though I owe almost nothing in financial indebtedness. So many people, living and dead, have contributed great benefits to my life—I could not possibly recount them all. I cannot even pay the interest on the principal they have invested in me.

As far as this modest book is concerned, I am in heavy debt to multitudes of authors who have written down their ideas and made them available to me. I am in heavy debt to preachers, teachers and associates who have poured much truth into my mind throughout my Christian life. I am in heavy debt to the men who have been willing to call themselves "disciples" through the years, and their numbers have now accelerated beyond my fondest dreams. I am in heavy debt particularly to men like Dom Fosco, who patiently edited and re-formatted these pages several times; and Clint Davis, who wrote (from notes and a tape) the chapter on the Prologue of Luke's Gospel. Most of all, I am in heavy debt to my precious wife, Judy, who serves also as a co-laborer and secretary, for loving and supporting me in her gentle and genuine way, and for adding her large wisdom to my small supply.

To these and many others, I give my deepest admiration and appreciation. How they all have blessed me! I repeat, they leave me in heavy debt. Thanks, friends. Herb Hodges

Table of Contents

Chapter1
How Vital is Vision?

"Where there is no vision, the people perish." Proverb 29:18

In spiritual terminology, "Divine perspective", "wisdom", "insight", "illumination", and "vision" are roughly equivalent terms. Many passages in the Word of God reveal the importance of such vision. Psalm 119:18 says, "Open Thou mine eyes, that I may behold wondrous things out of Thy Law." Psalm 119:130 says, "The entrance of Thy words giveth light, it giveth understanding unto the simple." James 1:5 says, "If any of you lack wisdom, let him ask of God." In Ephesians 1:15-19 and the context, Paul recorded one of the greatest of his prayers. I personally believe it is the most important prayer one human being can pray for another. It is a prayer for "illumination", the one subjective essential for understanding the things of God after the New Birth. "Except a man be born again, he cannot see." The two indispensables for spiritual understanding are regeneration and illumination.

The text of this study shows us negatively how important "vision" is. An individual's seeing depends on the "lens" he looks through, just as his hearing depends of the "filter" he listens through. As we begin this study of the Master's Great

Mandate to His people, it is necessary that we understand the value of vision. Proverbs 29:18 says, "Where there is no vision, the people perish." This is a cosmopolitan verse; it applies universally and absolutely.

A SPIRITUAL CONCEPT

Think, first, of the *spiritual concept* that is presented here, the concept of "vision." When viewed in context, it is evident that the vision that is mentioned is of a specialized kind. The reference is to spiritual vision, the most important kind of vision a person can have.

Everything begins with vision. You will be what you see, but what you do not see, you cannot be. You will become what you behold, but what you do not behold, you cannot become. In other words, what you look at lovingly, longingly, and lastingly, you will become like. You will be like what you look at.

This is clearly seen in the electronics world today. If you leave a single image on a computer screen long enough, it will burn its way into the computer tube, and will bleed through into any program that is called up thereafter. The principle holds for you as well: What you lastingly look at will determine your life.

A Louisiana Cajun had put his mule up for sale. A prospective buyer asked, "Are there any problems with the mule?" The Cajun answered, "Only that he don't look so good." The man answered, "Well, I don't really care about that. Does he work hard?" "Oh, yea, he work hard, he jus' don't look so good." So the man bought the mule, and the Cajun loaded him onto the new owner's trailer. When he arrived at his farm, he put down the ramp and brought the mule off the trailer. The mule immediately ran into a tree, then into the side of the barn. The farmer cried angrily, "I've been cheated! This mule is blind!" He reloaded the mule onto the trailer, went back to the original owner, and loudly exclaimed, "You misrepresented this mule to me. This mule is blind. You lied to me!" "Oh, no," the Cajun replied, "I don't lie to you. I tol' you, 'He don't look so good'!" Friends, everything depends on how good we look, how well we see.

Oswald Chambers, the renowned author of ***My Utmost For His Highest*** and other great devotional works, wrote with great perception when he said, "*It is easier to serve God without a vision, easier to work for God without a call, because then you are not bothered by what God requires; common sense is your guide, veneered over with Christian sentiment. But if once you truly hear the full commission of Jesus Christ, the awareness of what God wants will be your goal from that point on, and you will no longer be able to work for Him on the basis of common sense.*" Read this paragraph several times before proceeding further in this study. The italics in the paragraph are mine, not the author's.

Physical vision is a combination of objective stimulus (something real in the surrounding world) and subjective experience (the way the individual *perceives* the objective stimulus). The objective stimulus may never change, but once it registers upon the eyes of the individual, it is subject to distortion, rejection, or reception–in short, it is subject to the interpretation of the person upon whom the stimulus acts.

Of the five natural senses, vision is the one an individual can least afford to lose. Ralph Sockman was right when he picturesquely said, "The eye is the pope of the senses." Claud Monet, the famed French painter, said, "I am the absolute prisoner of my eyes." To a large degree, this is true of every man. Perception is the stimulus of everything. This formula will prove true: *Perception* leads to *Process* (or Procedure), and *Process* will lead to *Product.* In the church of Jesus Christ, it is apparent that we suffer at large from a radical crisis of product. We simply are not generally producing the kind of Christians who produced the Book of Acts! Thus, if our product is deficient, our perception must be deficient, also.

What is spiritual vision? The J. B. Phillips paraphrase of Colossians 1:9 defines it for us. Paul wrote, "I pray that you will see things from God's point of view." *Spiritual vision is seeing things from God's point of view.* But the Bible plainly tells us that His viewpoint will not agree with ours (Isaiah 55:10). Thus, a radical spiritual adjustment is necessary to bring our viewpoint into agreement with God's viewpoint.

Dawson Trotman, a man of great spiritual vision, said, "Vision is getting on your heart what God has on His." But what does God have on His heart? Our text answers that question in one word: "people." God has *people* on His heart. How *many* people? *All* people. God has on His heart every person on earth. And He expects His children to come into agreement with His concern.

He seriously expects His children to impact the whole wide world. Thus, a *global mission* requires a *global vision.* This means that most Christians need an "Atlas attack" in which they begin to see their responsibility to carry the whole world in order to begin to impact it for Christ.

Ponder the question again: What does God have on His heart? What should be at the heart of the believer's dreams and visions? The text answers: *people*. "Where there is no vision, *people* perish." Why, then, are 4/5 of the world's people only very poorly evangelized and very poorly educated in the substance and strategy of the Gospel, with nearly half of the human race never having redemptively heard the name of Jesus? Would the kind of Christianity revealed in the Book of Acts have tolerated this situation? Certainly not! Then what is the difference between the Christianity of the Book of Acts and the version of Christianity that largely prevails in today's evangelical (particularly American) church? Is the Jesus of today's church a different Jesus from theirs? No. Is the Holy Spirit different? No. Is the Bible different? Yes, but the advantage at this point lies with *us*, *not* with the early Christians. *They* didn't even *have* a completed New Testament. We do, but even with this advantage, we are nowhere near their impact level.

So what is the difference between the Christianity that produced the Book of Acts and *ou*r kind of Christianity? At the risk of over-simplification, it is my measured opinion that the only basic difference between "their Christianity" and "ours" is one of *strategy*. Their strategy showed an apparent disregard for building *institutions* and majored almost exclusively on building *individuals*. Their strategy was one of *explosion* (outward) instead of *implosion* (inward). Jesus trained twelve men, "whom He named apostles," (Luke 6:13). Why did He give a different name to them? What profile, what highlight, what insight is intended when His main (you *could* say His *only*) training process was centered in twelve men, and when He turns from the typical word "disciple" to give them the different and special title of "Apostle"? The key is surely in the meaning of the word. It is a compound Greek word, created by the joining of two smaller words. "Stolos" (the "stles" part of the word) means "to send." "Apo," the smaller prefixed preposition, means "Away from." Here lies the key. He built those specially chosen men to keep them "with Him" (Mark 3:14) *only long enough to train and infect them with His Life, His Vision, and His* ***Strategy***, and then it was His Design to send them as far away from their training base as they *could*, or *would*, or *might* go. His direction was: Temporarily *in*, but Vocationally *out*! And the fact that the list of Gifts (Gifted Men) He gave to His Church begins with "apostles" (Ephesians 4:11) indicates that the apostle was given to the church to turn the members and the ministry of the church *outward.*

It is my firm conviction that Jesus Christ fully expects every saved person to be dominated by a vision that is always turning his eyes and his feet out–to the ends of the earth. He clearly gave us a *global mission*, but (I repeat) a global vision certainly requires a *global vision.* And I also believe that both the vision and the vocation are to be *individual* and not primarily *institutional.* The "inactive" Christian of today's church, uninvolved in the task of world impact, is inconceivable and intolerable in the plan of God. I believe that Jesus fully expects every saved person to have a vision and a *strategy* (a strategy that was first clearly modeled by Him) to impact the world to the ends of the earth and until the end of time!

Remember that God has all people on His heart, and He expects no less of us. Henrietta Mears, the great Christian teacher, said, "When I consider my ministry, I think of the whole wide world. Anything less than that would not be worthy of Christ nor His will for my life." *A Christian without such a vision is like a spaceship that has lost its flight plan.* Its very momentum will cause it to arrive somewhere, but its intended goal can be dismissed if it refuses to operate by its flight plan. As Christians, our "flight plan" has always been one which calls for *Total World Impact*, and its specific strategy is decreed in our Lord's Great Commission. Anything less than this is man-made, and is not big enough to satisfy God.

It is a crucial insight to realize that when the Holy Spirit came on the day of Pentecost in the full release of redemptive power, the first stated outcome of His Coming was that "your young men shall see visions and your old men will dream dreams" (Acts 2:17). This has been twisted quite often into something so mystical, so mysterious, that it is confined to recluse mystics or psychic seers, but the truth is that this is to be the normal experience of spiritual Christians. According to the context, these visions and dreams are not those experienced in sleep, but those experienced by a heart which is filled with the Holy Spirit. In context, these dreams and visions are *strategy* dreams and visions which will lead toward the more complete fulfillment of our Lord's Great Commission. Such strategy dreams and visions should be the daily stock-in-trade of normal New Testament Christians, not the nebulous, mystical exceptions for a few flighty people.

I was teaching at a church leaders' retreat in a western state some years ago when a layman told me this story. He pointed to a fourteen-story building and repeated something which had been told about the corporate leaders there:

"That building houses a wealthy corporation. Sometime ago, several top leaders of the corporation went to the president and asked, 'What has the first vice-president got on you that requires you to retain him? Why do you pay him such a fabulous salary when he is so non-productive?' When the president asked them what they meant, they led him into the first vice-president's office and pointed through the small window which

looked into the workroom. The first vice-president was leaning back in a swivel chair which was turned away from his desk. His hands were behind his head and his feet were resting on the window sill. He was unmoving, either asleep or staring out the windows. 'See what we mean? That's all he ever does, and yet he draws a fabulous salary. Why?' The president soberly replied, 'Listen closely to me. Last year, that man in that seat in that office had one idea that netted this corporation over $85 million . . . This year, he has only one assignment . . . !'"

Dear fellow believers, where is the man in today's church who is thinking God's 85 million dollar idea? Where is the man who is seeing God's 85 million dollar vision, or dreaming God's 85 million dollar strategy dream? The Creator-God of the Bible never lacks giant creative ideas, but where are His common saints who are seeing from His viewpoint *strategically*, and getting on their hearts *strategically* what God has on His?

Let me state another formula concerning vision:
No vision = total failure;
Limited vision = little success;
A vision - a plan - action = only a dream;
A vision + a plan - action = a haunting dream (guilt); but
A vision + a plan + action = a spiritually productive ministry.

Note that the test of a person's vision is in the action that is stimulated by the vision. Without action, both you and your gifts will remain in the category of "potential." *Potential is dormant ability that is never mobilized through vision.*

Christian leader Myles Munroe, in a book entitled ***Understanding Your Potential***, said this about a believer's potential: "The wealthiest spot on this planet is not the oil fields of Kuwait, Iraq or Saudi Arabia. Neither is it the gold and diamond mines of South Africa, the uranium mines of the Soviet Union or the silver mines of Africa. Though it may surprise you, the richest deposits on our planet lie just a few blocks from your house. They rest in your local cemetery or graveyard. Buried beneath the soil there are dreams that never came to pass, songs that were never sung, books that were never written, paintings that never filled a canvas, ideas that were never shared, visions that never became reality, inventions that were never designed, plans that never went beyond the drawing board of the mind and purposes that were never fulfilled. Our graveyards are filled with massive volumes of potential that remained potential.

"Potential demands that you never settle for what you have accomplished. One of the great enemies of your potential is success. Small successes destroy great possibilities! In order to realize your full potential, you must never be satisfied with your last accomplishment. It is also important that you never let what you *cannot* do interfere with what you *can* do. The greatest tragedy in life is not death, but a life that never realized its full potential.

"To simplify this concept let us look at one of the most powerful elements in nature . . . the seed. If I held a seed in my hand and asked you, 'What do I have in my hand?' what would you say? Perhaps you would answer what seems to be the obvious . . . a seed. However, if you understand the nature of a seed, your answer would be *fact* but not *truth.* The truth is that I hold a forest in my hand. You see, in every seed there is a tree, and in every tree there are fruits or flowers with seeds in them. And these seeds also have trees that have fruit that have seeds . . . that have trees that have fruit that have seeds, etc., etc. What you see is not all there is. So the margin of difference between one seed and a food supply of wheat which could feed the whole world is called 'potential.' 'Potential' is the margin of difference between what you see and what could be.

"Suppose Shakespeare had died as an infant before he wrote his poems and plays - the potential of Macbeth would have been buried. Suppose Michelangelo had died before he painted the Sistine Chapel or DaVinci the Mona Lisa–the beauty of these paintings would have been lost. Suppose Mozart had died with all that music in his bosom.

"Suppose Moses had died before he saw the burning bush . . . or Paul before he met Jesus on the Damascus Road . . . or Abraham before Isaac was born. How different the pages of Scripture and history would be. Suppose Martin Luther had died without writing the theses . . . or Charles Wesley without penning his great hymns. . . or John Wycliff without translating the Bible into English. How different the history of the Church might have been.

"I wonder what would have happened if your father had died before you were conceived or your mother before you were born. What would the world have lost if you had not been born? What will the world lack because you fail to live out your potential? Will you carry songs, books, inventions, cures or discoveries to your grave?" The italics in this paragraph are mine, not the author's.

Could it be that the greatest sin of Christians lies in their unrealized potential? And the greatest unrealized potential today lies in the area of the fulfillment of the Great Commission of our Lord. He has assigned to you a specific role in Total World Impact, and it is a far greater role than you have yet played. This role will never be played without a vision of its possibility. ***So the most important thing in your life is to have and pursue a vision that agrees with God.*** Because your assignment is global, your vision must also be global. Do you have such a vision?

How do petty, self-oriented, provincial, parochial people like you and me gain God's vision? Here is a workable formula: *proper information* plus *spiritual illumination* will produce *vision*, which in turn will produce *motivation*, and this motivation will lead to *spiritually productive action*. Note that vision begins with proper information. Just as physical vision begins with the presentation of an external stimulus, so spiritual vision begins with the truth of God in Scripture and all that Scripture relates to. The "building blocks" for such vision are: a working knowledge of Scripture and a sensitive heart to hear it and obey it, an awareness of world geography and national and ethnic cultures of the world, a spiritual appraisal of current events, prayer, informative reading, first-hand experience (the "come and see" of Scripture) of some of the world's mission fields, fellowship with visionary believers, sacrificial giving to missionary causes, meeting productive missionaries and world-impacting Christians, and lifestyle choices. You can begin to cooperate with God in building spiritual vision into your life today. But it is tragically obvious that most Christians you fellowship with regularly do not have such a vision.

THE SAD CONDITION

Think, secondly, of the *sad condition* that is specified here. "Where there is no vision." The word "where" might be paraphrased "wherever," so this is a universal statement. What does "no vision" mean in Biblical terms? It means that there is no awareness of God and His Perfect Plan. It means that Satan, "the god of this world," has "blinded the minds of men" to the only things that really and ultimately count! They cannot see or understand these things without regeneration and/or illumination (see I Corinthians 2:9-14). Thus, there is no continuous traffic between heaven and the hearts of men. There is no commerce with that which is invisible, eternal, spiritual–and real. There is no listening to God and looking to Him. In short, "no vision" means that men do not see "the High and Holy One, Who inhabits Eternity," so we are limited to our little horizons and our selfish, petty, sinful plans. Such a limited person with such limited plans will finally implode into himself altogether. You see, everything begins with true vision. Please note the word "true". I use it in contrast to no vision, false vision, and limited vision.

We must sadly admit that most saved people are nearly as introverted, self-centered and survival-dominated as are lost people. In a word, most saved people are about as sinful (interpret "S-I-N" as Self-Ish-Ness) as are lost people. Why? Our text again provides the reason: No vision. We seldom see things "from God's point of view." We seldom have on our hearts what God has on His–a whole world of individual lost people.

The business community and others have recently employed a concept-word that echoes the Biblical concept of vision. The word is "paradigm." A person's seeing depends on the lens he looks through just as his hearing depends on the filter he listens through. This lens and filter comprise a person's "paradigm." Let me give an example of a paradigm.

To a child, spinach is the ultimate punishment; but to Popeye, spinach is the ultimate nourishment.

There are two paradigms revealed in that sentence–the child's paradigm, and Popeye's paradigm. The paradigm of each will totally determine how each person will see and understand spinach. To the child, spinach is "Yuk!" "Why are all the vitamins in yukky stuff instead of chocolate candy?" one child asked. But to Popeye, who has a different agenda and strategy (to whip Bluto and "win" the fair lady), spinach is necessary for energy and victory–and the taste is almost totally unimportant. This is a classic example of a paradigm.

Here is another example:

In the year 1877, an American astronomer named Percival Lowell impacted the scientific community with the theory that, on the basis of evidence he had accumulated, there was intelligent life on the planet Mars. The theory was partially based on his observations of "canals" on the surface of the planet. The theory took the scientific community by storm. However, there were a few people who knew early on that there were no canals on Mars. Mr. Lowell developed a serious health problem, and began to show symptoms of it. A team of physicians examined him and discovered the problem. The particular disease was so unknown in that day that they named it after him, calling it "Lowell's Syndrome." One particular symptom was noteworthy: When he sat for a particular time examining any object, the size and shape of the blood vessels in his eyes would be projected onto the surface of the object. So, instead of seeing "canals" on Mars through the telescope, he was actually seeing his own blood vessels! He "carried" what he thought he was observing outside himself in his own head. This is a classic example of a paradigm.

Here is yet another example:

Dr. Harold Lindsell, the editor emeritus of ***Christianity Today*** *news magazine, attended a Japanese eye clinic many years ago. While in class one day, the lecturer suddenly raised a chart before the class. He asked, "How many of you see the number eight?" Lindsell was the only one in the class who raised his hand at this point. He later said that he thought it was a conspiracy, that the entire class had intended to play a trick on him. But then, the lecturer asked, "How many of you see the number fourteen?" Every other person in the class raised a hand! The teacher spoke to Mr. Lindsell, "Sir, has anyone ever pointed out to you how seriously color-blind you are?" You see, there was no deceit involved. Every person in the class that day was telling the truth–as he saw it. One man actually saw the number eight while all the others saw the number fourteen. This is a classic example of a paradigm.*

You see, a paradigm blots out from vision everything that is not accommodated, and causes the vision to be totally dominated by that which is accommodated. So one's paradigms are all-important.

A lady approached Dr. G. Campbell Morgan, a great Bible teacher of the past, and said to him, "Dr. Morgan, do you really believe that God is interested in the little things in our lives?" Dr. Morgan replied gently, "Madam, you surely don't believe that anything in your life is big to God, do you?" Again, a paradigm.

I live in a college town. Recently, the standing joke I heard from the campus concerned the "bright" student who suddenly began failing all his courses. Upon investigation, it was discovered that he was using a black magic marker as his highlight pen!

This is what a paradigm does. It dismisses certain data as irrelevant, and elevates other data to the position of "truth." However, a paradigm may be so totally subjective (self-determined) that it has no basis in objective reality at all. Indeed, the paradigm may not even allow objective reality.

Let me give a Biblical example of a paradigm. *The thirteenth chapter of the book of Numbers records the story of the nation of Israel at Kadesh-Barnea, just south of the land God had promised them. They were apparently ready to enter the land. However, they balked in unbelief and sent a team of twelve spies into the land to spy out its vulnerability. The spies came back with a divided report. All agreed that the land was occupied by residents who likely had no thought of giving it up. Ten of the spies, an overwhelming majority, recommended against possession of the land on the basis that the present inhabitants of the land "are stronger than we," and that the children of Israel looked like grasshoppers compared to giants when standing beside them. Two of the spies gave a "minority" recommendation. Admitting the same realities, they nonetheless said, "Let us go up at once and take possession, for we are well able to overcome it" (Numbers 13:30). You see, the minority group factored God into their conclusion while the majority did not. So two paradigms determined the different recommendations: one included God, the other did not.* ***All saw the "giants"; most saw themselves as "grasshoppers"; only two truly saw God. Rather, the majority saw God through the giants, and thus the giants looked bigger than God. The minority saw the giants through God, and thus God was bigger than the giants.*** So their perception determined their proposal and their performance. Herein lies the difference between "vision" and "no vision"!

Human intelligence will always give you your point of view. Only a miracle of illumination will give you God's point of view. Therein lies the difference between "no vision," without which "the people perish," and "vision," by means of which the people flourish.

Imagine no spiritual vision in the *pulpit* of the church you attend. Imagination is not required if you visit many churches! I Samuel 3:1 says, "The Word of God was precious (scarce) in those days, and there was no open (frequent) vision." A reading of the national history that ensued from this point will reveal that tragic things resulted from such a loss of vision.

What if there were no Gospel preached in the pulpit of your church? No awareness of man's lostness without Christ? No trust in the transforming power of the Holy Spirit? No unfolding of the deep, rich, eternal counsels of God? No exposure of the infinite riches hidden in the Word of God? No equipping of the listeners to "live in heaven and on earth at once"? No teaching of the vast vocation of the Spirit-filled, Word-adapted, prayer-oriented, disciple-building Christian life? Imagine a pulpit with "no vision".

Pastor, to what degree are you in doubt about the effectiveness of what you are presently doing? Wholesome doubt is the hammer that breaks the windows that are clouded with human fancies. That wholesome doubt is a very hopeful sign. Without an honest admission of such doubt and a prayerful investigation of the Divine alternative, the pulpit you occupy may continue void of vision.

Some years ago, a great Southern Baptist pastor was praying prostrate on the floor of his study one morning, asking God for an anointing of the Holy Spirit's power upon his ministry. Over and over, he passionately pleaded with God, "Lord, give me Your power. Do not let me preach and minister without Your power." Every serious preacher has prayed this prayer with earnest appeal. However, he declared that suddenly it seemed that the roof over him opened and a hand came down and touched his shoulder and it seemed that God's voice spoke within him, saying, "My son, stop praying!" When he became quiet, the Voice seemed to clearly say, "My son, with plans no bigger than yours, you don't need My power!"

Christian, is your vision God-big for His glory? Where are the plans, the dreams, the visions, the strategies for total world impact that truly tax the miracle resources of God? Where is the strategy that requires ongoing miracles for its sustenance? Where is the vision that is so big that human resources (whatever the kind or amount) cannot possibly sponsor it? The only eternity-sized vision any of us will ever need is in the Great Commission given to us by the Lord Jesus Christ. If your pulpit is not obsessed with the terms "make disciples" and "all nations," how can God possibly be expected to put Heaven's approval upon it? Without this magnificent obsession, the pulpit of your church is marked by "no vision."

Then, it is only a short step to a *pew*, a people, with no spiritual vision of these things. A rule of inner church life is, "like pastor, like people". The people will gradually take on the spiritual profile of their pastor. Suppose, in this succession, that the people in the pew did not have, or lost, their vision of the supernal glory of the Gospel? And of the absolute magnificence of Jesus Christ? And of the greatness and glory of our worldwide task? And of the possibility of impacting the whole wide world with Jesus Christ and His

Gospel as the early Christians did? Someone truly said, "The steps from risktaker to caretaker to undertaker are very short steps."

Why do church members get much more excited about a thousand other things than about God, spiritual things, heaven, hell, and eternity? The answer? No vision, thus no motivation, because motivation arises out of vision.

Careful study of the Gospels and the Book of Acts will disclose that the typical Christian Church is run far more on the basis of tradition than on the basis of illumination. Someone wryly said, "Churches had better do and say everything right the first time, because they are going to do it the same way from now on."

When the loss of vision occurs in pulpit and pew, we may be sure that there will be no spiritual vision in *public life.* What if Christians totally lost the vision of their role as salt and light (Matthew 5:14-16) in a decaying and dark world? What if we lost our vision of ourselves as "bodily substitutes", or representatives, of Jesus Christ (II Corinthians 5:20), "in the midst of a crooked and perverse generation, among whom we shine as lights in the world, holding forth the Word of Life" (Philippians 2:14-16)? What if we lost our vision of our high status as "ambassadors for Christ", commissioned to mediate our King's cause in this dark and alien world? But we don't have to guess about it. The absence of vision is clearly observable in pulpit, pew, and public life–merely by examining the occurrence of the consequences declared in this text.

THE SERIOUS CONSEQUENCES

Think of the *serious consequences* that follow the sad condition of "no vision". "Where there is no vision, the people perish." The word translated "perish" is a most revealing Hebrew word. It is frighteningly full. It has several different meanings. It means "to cast off restraint, to loosen, to dissolve, to break up, to go to pieces, to go naked, to perish." So look at the tragic consequences of a loss of vision among Christians.

First, when there is no vision, the people of the society, of the community, of the church, of the home, "*cast off restraint*". This is the *moral* effect of a loss of vision. A loss of vision produces moral anarchy, in which "every man does what is right in his own eyes." Incidentally, note that when there is no awareness of ultimate reality, men do what is "right in their own eyes", not necessarily what is apparently wrong to them. Remember, too, that "right" and "wrong" are always relative terms to those with merely natural or carnal minds. "Right" and "wrong" are absolutes only to those with a truly spiritual mind. "There is a way that seems right to a man, but the end of it is death" (Proverbs 14:12). Note that the man is certain that his way is *right*; he never dreams that his way is Satanic and destructive. Again, the difference is in the revelation, the vision, the perception of the individual. It is absolutely amazing to observe how people who are totally blind to spiritual reality give total credibility to their own understanding!

That men everywhere today have cast off restraint is agreed by everyone. Autonomy, anarchy, and self-determination are increasingly wide-spread. The difference between the Son of God and sinners is evident at this point. Jesus said, "I do always the things which please my Father" (John 8:29), but the motto of sinners (indeed, the essence of sin) is, "I do always those things which please me." Some future sculptor may picture twentieth century man with his arms wrapped about himself in loving embrace, kissing his own image in a mirror. However, lest the tragic seriousness of such a situation be absorbed in mild humor, let the words which John Milton placed in the lips of Satan in ***Paradise Lost*** correct us. Satan showed the inevitable acknowledgment of sinners who pursue their selfishness without restraint when he said, "Myself am hell."

Some years ago, the newspapers carried the story of a twenty-year-old mechanic's helper at Idlewild Airport in New York. He wrote a letter to a friend in the air force in Texas. The letter told how the young man had broken off with his girl friend, and how he planned to take one of the Pan American planes. He stole a twin-engine DC-3 and sent it roaring down the runway. It failed to gain altitude, crashed, and he was killed. The news item closed with his words from the letter, "I'll be on my own at the controls, just like I've always been–alone." This story is repeated again and again, in different clothes, every day–and it always comes out the same. To be self-managed is to be self-damaged. The self-managed person always crashes and burns! Because the ideas of men disagree so radically when each is a law unto himself, world tensions continue to mount. Where there is no frequent vision among men, no clear word from the living God, no vital Christianity, then the people cast off restraint.

Second, this strong Hebrew verb also means *"to disintegrate."* "Where there is no vision, the people *disintegrate*." This is the *social* effect of a loss of vision. Sin, which increases proportionately in a society with the loss of spiritual vision, has a centrifugal force about it, driving men outward from the True Center of Life, God Himself, and thus driving them from each other. So we have a fragmented, divided world. Society begins to "loosen, dissolve, break up, go to pieces." The word "split" is used to describe many situations in our world. We have split atoms, split families, split nations, a split world, and split personalities. A psychiatrist pulled into a service station one day driving a pickup truck. In the back of the truck were three chairs. When asked where he was going, he replied, "I'm going to visit a schizophrenic!" How often individuals are "going to pieces". A college girl said to her roommate, "I feel like a walking Civil War." Her roommate replied, "That's nothing, I'm a walking *World* War!" An individual can weather almost any problem if he is inwardly united, but he is vulnerable to any attack if he is in controversy with himself.

The story of Judas in the New Testament concludes with these words: "Now this man purchased a field with the reward of iniquity; and falling headlong, he burst asunder in the midst, and all his bowels gushed out" (Acts 1:18). As you know, Judas hanged himself, and this physical collapse resulted either from his ineptness in trying to hang himself, or as a result of the bloating and decay that resulted from his dead body hanging on the rope for some time. The Amplified Bible says, "He burst open in the middle of his body." As gruesome as this sounds, it gives us a perfect illustration. One translation says that Judas "disintegrated". He literally "came apart". But this was only a final, physical symptom of what had gradually happened for at least three years previous. He had displaced the only possible center, the Divine "cement", which would have integrated his personality and made it a unified whole. He really "went to pieces in the middle." And Judas could well be the "patron saint" of this age. The Bible tells us (Colossians 1:17) that in Jesus Christ alone do "all things hold together," but when men lose "the Beatific Vision of Jesus Christ", society has no cementing influence, no cohesive force, no integrating center.

In Marc Connally's play, **Green Pastures***, the angel Gabriel has been striding the ramparts of heaven, becoming more and more disturbed by the chaos and turmoil he witnesses on the earth. Finally, he turns to God and says, "Lawd! Lawd! It looks like everything nailed down is a-coming loose!" Individuals and institutions disintegrate when Christ is not in control.* This is the social result of a loss of spiritual vision.

Third, this Hebrew word also means "*to be unclothed,*" or "*to go naked.*" Presumably, since every other use of the word is spiritual in nature, this meaning is also spiritual. What a rich field of Biblical study is opened to us if we see this meaning as applying to the spiritual condition of human beings. The translation, "the people are unclothed," reveals the *personal* effect of no vision. Consistently throughout the Bible, the saving of sinners, their "justification," is seen in terms of their being "clothed" with the protecting and qualifying righteousness of Christ, and their condemnation and judgment are seen in terms of their being unclothed and exposed to judgment. In fact, throughout the Bible, clothing is a picture of both sin and righteousness. Dirty clothes are often used as a picture of sin and self-righteousness, and clothes clean and white are used as a picture of the covering, qualifying righteousness of Christ. If you wish to pursue this idea further on the pages of Scripture, these passages will prove to be a rich and rewarding field of study: Genesis 3:7, 21; Zechariah 3:1-5; Matthew 22:11-13; Luke 15:22; Romans 13:11-14; Ephesians 4:22-24; Colossians 3:5-14; and Revelation 19:7-8.

One of the happiest things in being a Christian is in knowing that God has dressed me in Heaven's Best Garment–and at His own expense! This is reflected in John Bunyan's famous classic Christian allegory, **Pilgrim's Progress***. When the convicted pilgrim comes to the Cross of Jesus and trusts Him, the* *burden of his sin falls from him and he rises in celebration of forgiveness and eternal life. He is then met on the road by "Three Shining Ones," who represent God the Father, God the Son, and God the Holy Spirit. God the Father says to the converted pilgrim, "Peace be unto thee. Thy sins are forgiven." God the Son strips off the dirty garments the pilgrim was wearing and replaces them with a bright white clean robe. And God the Holy Spirit places a mark on his forehead (representing the seal of the Holy Spirit), and a rolled-up scroll in his hand (representing the Bible).*

It is that second work, the work of stripping and reclothing the sinner that is in mind when our text says, "Where there is no vision, the people are unclothed." John 3:36 says, "He who believes on the Son has everlasting life, but he who believes not the Son shall not see life, but the wrath of God abides on him." The believer who is trusting Christ is covered by the righteousness of Christ and escapes the wrath of God against sin, but the unbelieving sinner is unclothed, and thus fully exposed to every force that will destroy him.

"Where there is no vision," more and more people remain "unclothed," or unprotected for time and eternity. This is the personal consequence of no vision.

Finally, the Hebrew word is accurately translated in the King James Version. It means to "*perish*". "Where there is no vision, the people perish." Compassion is surely called for here, simply because the commodity in danger is "people". If it were animals or plants, it would not be nearly so serious. But it is people, individuals like you and me. They "perish". In John 3:16, the word "perish" is placed in antithesis to having "everlasting life". To perish means to be involved forever in a living death and a dying life in a place called hell.

Meanwhile, I Corinthian 1:18 indicates that people without Christ are in a *present* state of perishing. This perishing of people is the spiritual and eternal effect of a loss of vision by Christians. Three people every second perish without Christ, and the Church has largely lost it's vision! Hell fills, and Heaven has vacancies yet to be filled! All because the Church's vision has faded!

Years ago, a wealthy business man went to India on a Bengal tiger hunt. He was in India for six weeks. Upon his return home, he went to the mid-week service of the large church he attended. The church was discussing its annual budget. The businessman shocked the entire church by proposing that all foreign missions giving be omitted from the budget. An elderly gentleman asked the reason for this strange proposal. The reply was, "I have just returned from a six-week trip to India, and during that time, I did not see a single missionary." The older gentleman asked, "And what was the purpose of your trip to India?" The reply was, "I went there on a Bengal tiger hunting trip." "And how many Bengal tigers did you see?" "I saw six of them." The older man said, "That's very peculiar. I spent thirty years in India as a missionary, and I saw hundreds and hundreds of missionaries. But I have yet to see my first Bengal tiger in India!" So very, very much depends on our perspective and our vision.

The words of Proverbs 29:18 were written by King Solomon, a man in whose reign the vision faded. And there was no more disastrous failure in the history of Israel than that of Solomon. The people went to pieces! The nation collapsed! The Kingdom was divided!

The alternative before us is clear: it is either "*vision or division*"*!* This is true universally, nationally, locally, but especially is it true in the Church of Jesus Christ and in the individual Christian life!

We must, we *must*, wait upon God in quietness and prayer, armed with a deep sense of need and a teachable heart, and ask Him to restore the vision of His overwhelming Personal Glory, and of His overpowering Plan for us and the world! As the vision is restored, we will rediscover that His entire Plan is revealed in our Lord's Great Commission, and that the mandate there is to "turn people into disciples."

Dawson Trotman was right when he said, "Spiritual vision is getting on your heart what is on God's heart–the world!" Paul prayed that the Colossian Christians might "see things from God's point of view" (Colossians 1:9, Phillips). What a revolution would occur if we did!

"One man awake
 Can waken another;
The second can waken
 His next-door brother.
The three awake
 Can rouse a town
By turning the whole
 Place upside down
The many awake
 Can make such a fuss
That it finally awakens
 The rest of us.
One man up,
 With dawn in his eyes,
MULTIPLIES!"

Chapter 2
The Commission that Determines Our Mandate

"All power is given unto me in heaven and in earth. Go ye therefore, and teach all nations, baptizing them in the name of the Father, and of the Son, and of the Holy Ghost, teaching them to observe all things whatsoever I have commanded you; and, lo, I am with you alway, even unto the end of the world."

Matthew 28:18-20

When we leave home, we often state our most important instructions and affirmations just before we leave—things we don't want other people to forget. My wife posts them on the kitchen table or the kitchen counter or the refrigerator. What do they mean? This is important!

George Peters, in his book, ***A Biblical Theology of Missions***, wrote, "The Great Commission is our beacon light in the midst of human fog and conjecture. We desperately need a new and penetrating study of the Great Commission. Few teachers and commentaries deal exhaustively with the Great Commission passages. The church needs to seriously rethink the Commission to make disciples." Retired missionary John McGee, a career missionary to Nigeria, said, "There is more in the Great Commission than a person can dream about, or think about, or do about, even if he had ten lifetimes."

In the paragraph which includes the Great Commission (Matthew 28:16-20), we read that "the eleven disciples went away into Galilee, into a mountain where Jesus had appointed them." This is the only post-resurrection appearance of Jesus that is by previous appointment. The other appearances seem to have been somewhat "spontaneous." There was surely something very important that Jesus wanted to say or do on this occasion. And, indeed, there was! Here He "posted" His Final Instructions. We have a common saying among us, "When Everything Else Fails, Read the Instructions." In this chapter, we are going to read and study His Final Instructions. We will divide those instructions into two headings: The Assurance behind the Commission, and the Assignment within the Commission. If we are to understand and fulfill the Great Commission, we must carefully investigate these two things.

THE ASSURANCE BEHIND THE COMMISSION (V. 18, 20A)

The Commission opens with one of the most staggering announcements ever made. Jesus said, "All authority is given unto me in heaven and in earth." Both His credibility and our commission depend on that sentence. What does it mean, and how important is it?

The "authority" stated here is ***Divine*** authority. The great principle in all of Scripture is that "there is no authority except from God" (Romans 13:1), and that principle is certainly reflected here. The Greek word for authority is *exousia*, which literally means "out of being." Consider this carefully. It means that all of the necessary authority out of the very being of God is given to us through our association with Christ to fulfill this Commission.

Then this authority is ***delegated*** authority. Jesus Christ has an inherent authority in His Person, an authority He possesses in virtue of Who He is. The authority which He possessed during His earthly life was manifested in obvious ways.

He demonstrated His authority over nature when, with a word of His mouth and a gesture of His hand, He had silenced a raging storm that had become so wild that even professional fishermen were afraid. He had spoken to a fig tree and it withered before the bewildered eyes of the disciples.

He also had authority over the realm of human conscience. Using nothing greater as a weapon than a brief and simple conversation with her, our Savior awakened the conscience of a sin-stained Samaritan woman and set the strings of hope vibrating in her soul. On another occasion, while completely surrounded by an inquisitive crowd, using nothing but a mention of the man's name and an invitation to come down from a tree, He quickened the conscience of a despicable and Godless Jew of Jericho named Zacchaeus.

He also manifested during His earthly lifetime a supreme authority over that unseen spiritual world which is separated by just a thin veil from the material world. By a spoken word or a touch of the hand, He could dispel the principalities and powers of evil that had captured a man's life.

He also possessed a marvelous authority in the realm of human infirmity and disease. Using His power with no flare for the spectacular, but solely to aid the lives of ailing people, He made the deaf to hear, the blind to see, the dumb to speak, the lame to walk, twisted bodies to be made straight, and the dead to return to life again.

His teaching, too, was characterized by authority. After His first teaching in the synagogue, the people "were astonished at His teaching: for He taught them as one having authority, and not as the scribes" (Mark 1:22). Jesus had no hesitancy in assuming the completest authority. He claimed the authority to forgive sins (Mark 2:10). He made statements which modified the provisions of the law of Moses, which everyone accepted as of Divine origin (Matthew 5:21, 27, 33). He even claimed that He Himself would be each man's final judge (John 5:27).

But the authority reflected in these claims is not the authority referred to in Matthew 28:18. Jesus said that this particular authority "is given," apparently on the basis of His accomplishment in His Death and Resurrection. The authority which He now possessed in His resurrection glory far surpassed the authority He had had during His lifetime. Every kind of authority was now His. This authority had been given Him by the Divine decree of His Father in heaven. The disciples knew that they were servants of a Master whose authority upon earth and in heaven was beyond all question. Romans 1:4 says that "He was declared to be the Son of God with power (authority) . . . by the resurrection from the dead." It is this authority which forms the foundation of the Commission which He gives to His disciples.

What an astounding claim! A. T. Robertson said, "It is the most sublime spectacle in world history to see the Risen Christ, without money or army or state, charging this band of five hundred men and women with world conquest and bringing them to believe it was possible and to undertake it with serious passion and power."

Also, this authority is ***deserved*** authority. Jesus said, "All authority is given unto Me." Notice that this authority is not given to us, but to Him. However, this should not cause us distress, because whatever is His belongs to every saved person. Every born-again person is an heir of God because he is a "joint-heir with Christ" (Romans 8:17). Everything in the Father's estate which belongs rightfully to Christ now also belongs to me because of my faith-association, or faith-identification, with Him. Whatever is His is mine, not because I deserve it, but because I am in Him. Note, too, that this authority is not given to Him as Son of God. As God, nothing can be added to Him, and nothing can be taken away. The authority which Jesus claims here is an authority which He has gained (earned, merited, deserved) as Son of Man. The verb "was given" indicates a past act, and apparently refers to the actual investiture of this authority on the day of His resurrection from the dead. This corresponds to the great Humiliation-Exaltation passage in Philippians 2:5-11. After Paul had shown the dizzying humiliation of Jesus, he then reveals His resultant exaltation. "Wherefore, God also hath highly exalted Him, and given Him a name which is above every name: That at the name of Jesus every knee should bow, of things in heaven, and things in earth, and things under the earth; And that every tongue should confess that Jesus Christ is Lord, to the glory of God the Father" (Philippians 2:9-11). So both His exaltation and His authority were merited by His death and resurrection.

Finally, the authority He claimed before He gave His Great Commission was a clearly *defined* authority. "All authority is given unto Me in heaven and in earth." The two mentioned spheres are the only two areas in which we function, and as far as we know, they are the only two areas in which Jesus Christ functions. "In heaven and on earth." All celestial authority is His, and all terrestrial authority is His. He declares to His disciples that "all authority is given unto Me in heaven," where He has received "a Name which is above every name," where He has been "exalted to the right hand of power," where He has been "crowned with glory and honor." He announces also that "all authority has been given unto Me on earth." So He is the absolute Master of both worlds.

In Shakespeare's ***King Lear***, he pictures the Earl of Kent coming in disguise to the King. King Lear says, "What do you want?" The Earl of Kent answers, "I would serve you." King Lear asks, "Why?" Then comes the famous answer of the Earl of Kent, "Because there is that in your countenance that I would willingly call master." The King asks, "What is it?" The Earl of Kent replies, "Authority."

Jesus makes the legitimate claim that all authority is His. And it is in this authority that the missionary enterprise (and the disciple-making command) is to be carried out. His authority has not abated or decreased with the passing centuries. On the basis of that authority, we are to undertake the assignment given in the Commission.

THE ASSIGNMENT WITHIN THE COMMISSION (V.19, 20)

THE CHURCH'S (CHRISTIAN'S) ONLY MARCHING ORDERS

The Great Commission constitutes the only "marching orders" Jesus Christ ever gave to His Church. The Great Commission is a mandate to soul-winning and missions, but it is far more than that. There is a five-fold account of the Great Commission of our Lord in the New Testament. It is stated in different ways in Matthew 28:18-20 (the most definitive statement), Mark 16:15 (the most concise form), Luke 24:47, John 20:21, and Acts 1:8 (the most expansive interpretation).

In Matthew's account, the Church of Jesus Christ finds the basis of its task. There is absolutely no question in Matthew's statement about what Jesus intended His followers to do. It is not a matter of emotion or feeling. It is not a work to be carried on at our convenience. Jesus left specific instructions. These instructions are both ultimate (timeless and changeless) and immediate. The Commission is in effect right now, and binds every Christian to its fulfillment at this moment. The verbs of this Commission are words of action: Go, make disciples, baptize, and teach. Simply stated, the Church is under orders, but the exact nature of the orders may surprise most believers.

DIVISION OF THE COMMISSION INTO PARTS

I want to divide the Commission into seven parts. Here is the outline. First, we are responsible to *employ all available personnel* (the word "ye" of verse 19 is plural). Then, we are to *enter the field* of service ("go"). Third, we are to constantly *enlarge our vision* ("all nations"). Fourth, we are to *evangelize the prospects* ("make disciples"). Fifth, we are to *enlist the evangelized* ("baptizing them in the name of the Father, and of the Son, and of the Holy Ghost"). Sixth, we are to *educate and edify the enlisted* ("teaching them to observe all things whatsoever I have commanded you"). And finally, we are to *expect him to work* ("and lo, I am with you always, even to the end of the world"). So you see, there may be a great deal more to our Lord's Commission than we have honored!

As we seriously and carefully investigate the Commission, we make a startling discovery. We find that for approximately two centuries, the Commission worked to perfection and rapidly impacted the known world. But then a peculiar thing happened. Something went terribly wrong. In order to see this, I want to look at each of the seven points I have outlined. Under each point, I want you to think of two sub-headings. One is entitled "The Savior's Strategy," and the other is called "Satan's Substitute." We will do this with each of the seven outline points in the Commission.

1. EMPLOY THE PERSONNEL

The first point of the Commission is to *employ all the personnel.* In verse 19, the word "ye" is plural, and literally means "all of you."

The Savior's Strategy

Someone described Jesus' intention for the fulfillment of this Commission in these words: "All believers are to be at it, and they are to be *always* at it." The one thing, apart from the divine power, that made the Great Commission such a sweeping success at the beginning was that it marshalled its total work force to the point of service. The goal was that every disciple be a soul-winning, disciple-making reproducer of the same kind of reproducers. They were all propagandists and evangelists! In fact, participation was so universal among them that rules had to be made to avoid confusion (see I Cor. 14:31). There were no mere spectators or observers among them. Adolph Harnack, a great church historian, said, "When the church won its greatest victories in the early days of the Roman Empire, it did so not by teachers or preachers or apostles, but by amateur, informal missionaries." This Commission calls for a personal ministry *from every believer.* All the members of Christ's Body cannot do this unless each member does it. A church in modern Manhattan had this message on its church sign: "Pastor, ------." "Ministers: Every member of the congregation." This is the Savior's strategy for employing the personnel.

Satan's Substitute

Now look at Satan's substitute. The fact is that the Commission worked. It worked too well to suit Satan. It worked so well that it took him 200 years to recover and regroup his forces. Finally, he fought the Commission with a substitute program of his own. It is not difficult to see that the original Commission has been tampered with. It has been amended, and for long centuries, many churches have fallen for Satan's program. Satan's most important blow against the Commission was directed at this first point, to employ all the personnel.

Early in church history, Satan orchestrated a division of the Church into two groups, and he over-emphasized the distinctions. The large majority he called "the laity," and the small minority he began to call "the clergy." And his selling point was that laymen are not capable and gifted, and that they have no special interest in the real vocation of the church, anyway. So Satan presided over the creation of a hierarchy of professional religious men. These professional men were to (1) fight all the spiritual battles, and (2) do all the spiritual work. The business of the "layman"? To support the professional leader and to pay for his program to be fulfilled (in the New Testament, the *people are* the program).

So a "ladder of dedication" was formed within the Church. From the top of the ladder, there was the "missionary," then the pastor, then the other professional religious workers, and at the very bottom was the lowly layman. Someone has described our age as "the age of the spectator." Football has 22 players at one time, but it may have several million spectators! Baseball has 18 players at one time, basketball ten, boxing two, and some Olympic events only one. But all of these sports have millions of fans. Comic Fred Allen said, "If society continues the way it is going, we soon may have a world full of people with eyes the size of saucers, and brains the size of an English pea."

The Church's Unemployment and Underemployment Problems

The church has developed two "unemployment" problems, and the two problems constantly support each other, thus making the situation steadily worse. There is the problem of the *unemployment* of the *members* of the local church body. Because the average church member in the average church does not fulfill his Divinely-assigned job description, his "paycheck" is reduced to a welfare, subsistence ration. His responsibility is unfulfilled, his reward is forfeited, the world is left in darkness, and Satan is quite satisfied.

Then, there is the closely related problem of the *underemployment* of the *minister.* The typical pastor in today's church is overworked, but underemployed! When Henry M. Stanley returned from Africa and his renowned search for David Livingstone, a newsman asked him the facetious question, "What bothered you the most while you were in

Africa—the lions or the snakes?" To which Stanley wryly replied, "Neither! It was the gnats and the mosquitoes!" Our pastors hardly even see the lions and the tigers because they are constantly struggling with gnats and mosquitoes. While atomic wars are being fought in the spiritual realm, they are struggling to survive a barrage of popcorn! The red herring of multiplied exhausting religious activities and spurious false images of his job has been drawn across his path and he cannot fulfill the only job description God has given for his work.

Just this week, I received the report from a State Convention office that 300 Southern Baptist pastors per month are being forcibly ejected, dismissed, from pulpits of Southern Baptist churches. I cannot vouch for that number, but I do know that the problem is *extremely* serious. I also heard the report several years ago that over 1,000 Southern Baptist pastors a year are abandoning the pulpits of Southern Baptist churches. Neither can I prove that number, but I do know that *the problem is extremely serious!* Perhaps the greatest reason for this attrition of called leadership is that the leader is tragically unfulfilled by his "underemployment" situation.

Spectator Christianity in the Church

Inside the church, we have developed a spectator Christianity in which few speak and many listen. The church is filled with a "fraternity of fans," fans of the faith. Imagine a wholesale house which had a sales manager whose business was to sell the goods and to lecture on the quality of the goods and the mechanics of selling. Suppose it also had a large "selling staff" whose only real business was to enlist and encourage auditors to listen to the lectures of the sales manager.

What a monstrosity it would be! How long would it stay in business? James S. Stewart of Edinburgh, Scotland, said, "The real problem of Christianity is not atheism or skepticism, but the non-witnessing, non-productive Christian trying to smuggle his own soul into heaven all alone." This is Satan's strategy, and furthermore, he has worked so on that word "ye" until now not even all "clergy" are witnesses!

Look at the Christian community. *On which side does the typical church fall, on the side of the Savior's strategy, or on the side of Satan's substitute?* The answer is tragically apparent. We must re-examine our Marching Orders!

2. ENTER THE FIELD

The second point in our outline of the Commission is to *enter all the field.* The word "go" is an active, aggressive word, a word which entails movement.

The Savior's Strategy

The Savior's strategy is obvious. In Matthew 13:38, He said, "The field is the world." This is not the field for "the" church, *it is the field for your local church! Jesus Christ fully expects you to take on the whole wide world!* The symbols Jesus used for Christians and the Gospel are bound together by a common denominator. They are all characterized by the idea of penetration. Jesus used such symbols as light, salt, keys, bread, and water. Light is worthless unless it penetrates and dispels the darkness. Salt is no good if it remains in the box or the salt-shaker; it must penetrate the salad or the potatoes. One little boy said, "Salt is the stuff that spoils the potatoes—if you leave it out." Keys are useless unless they penetrate the lock. Bread has little value outside the eater, and water doesn't meet the thirsty man's need unless it penetrates into him.

Even so, Christians are to constantly penetrate the world.

Someone said, "You can't spell the word 'God' without the word 'go' in it; you can't spell the word 'good' without the word 'go' in it; you can't spell the word 'Gospel' without the word 'go' in it; and neither can you obey the Gospel and be a good servant of God unless you go—*on his terms.* Christianity is centrifugal in nature and thrust, and not primarily centripetal. Every Christian is to live vocationally (as a Christian) on a frontier of penetration, whether the frontier is a scientific laboratory, a library, a factory, a fruit orchard, a delivery route, an executive desk, a space-age jetliner, a psychiatrist's clinic, or a pastor's study. Our "world" is wherever we are with people. In Luke 10:1-3, the Bible tells us that "the Lord appointed seventy, and *sent them two by two before his face into every city and place whither he himself would come.* Therefore He said unto them, The harvest truly is great, but the laborers are few. *Pray therefore the Lord of the harvest that he would send (thrust) forth laborers into his harvest.* Go your ways: behold, *I send you forth as lambs among wolves.*" Note carefully the units of words which I have emphasized. What a world is in these verses! Every Christian is to be a trailblazer, a forerunner, for the coming of Christ "into every place whither He Himself would come." Lambs among wolves can only hope to survive by a miracle!

Incidentally, the word "go" in the Commission is NOT a COMMAND. To regard it as a command is to advance "the ladder of Christian dedication" concept. If it were a command, anyone who went to some distant place to preach the Gospel or to witness for Christ would be regarded as special. But the verb means, "As you are going," or even, "Since you are going." Jesus would never be so senseless as to command us to do something that we are already doing! Where is your church on Tuesday afternoon at three? Is it in the church building? No, it is "*going*." The issue is not: Why doesn't the church get out into the world? It is rather: Is the church performing its assignment as it penetrates?

A few years ago, I was in a large, beautiful city in a foreign country. I preached at the English-speaking church there on Sunday morning. I arrived considerably early so I could visit with the people as they arrived. I received quite a shock from the people. Most of the Americans were employees of an international oil company and had high-salaried jobs. When I asked how they were enjoying their time there, they all complained of monotony and boredom. Many of them were there for two-year assignments. In my message, I asked why they didn't learn the language and/or arm themselves with Gospel tracts printed in the language of the people and practice missions, evangelism, and soul-winning while they were there. They disregarded this possibility apparently without a second thought! You see, someone has sold us a "bill of goods" that leads to a radical betrayal of Jesus and His Commission. They had "gone" (even financed by an oil company), but they had no awareness of their responsibility "as they were going."

Satan's Substitute

Satan has intruded a subtle substitute into the mentality of the Church. Two of the greatest of Gospel words are "come" and "go." Once we have come to Christ (Matthew 11:28-30, for example), we are to "go and tell" all men what we have found in Christ. Satan is a master manipulator and twister of words. He induced a slow perversion in the Church from "go and tell" to "come and hear." One Socialist observer caricatured the Church in these words: "The motto of Christians seems to be, 'Come here, and get God's message, and go to heaven, or stay away, and go to hell'!" Paul Little said, "The problem is not that the *gospel* has lost its *power*; the problem is that the *church* has lost its *audience*." Another said, "The Holy Spirit cannot save saints and seats—yet the Church is full of both!"

Consider a medical analogy. Suppose the Department of Health feared an epidemic of scarlet fever. What would it do to stop the spread of the disease? It would isolate the germ-carriers. It would quarantine the infected, and thus the fever would be contained. Suppose the Department of *hell* wanted to stop an epidemic of New Testament Christianity. It would surely do everything possible to isolate the "carriers," and thus stop the spread. And that is precisely what has happened in the Church at large. We have developed a kind of "holy huddle" inside the Church. The team never seems to get "into the trenches" at the line of scrimmage, where the game must be played if victory is to be the result. And some like the coziness and safety of this arrangement. After all, did you ever hear of a football player getting hurt in the huddle? So we plan our strategy, analyze the enemy, recite "chalk-talks," and even criticize our own team members. We worry about membership, programs, buildings and finances. We have weekly "dress parades," and our key command seems to be "as you were." Forgive the mixture of metaphors, but you surely get the message. We are constantly multiplying our religious activities, perfecting our organizational programs, expanding and developing our denominational institutions, and strengthening our ecclesiastical structures, and all in the world we are doing in many, many church situations is *maintaining and entertaining ourselves! The devil must be awfully happy!* The typical church operates almost exclusively by his substitute instead of the Savior's strategy.

3. ENLARGE THE VISION

The third point in our Lord's Commission is to constantly *enlarge the vision.* "All nations" is the field of activity in the Commission.

The Savior's Strategy

Let us remind ourselves again—Jesus Christ is not playing games with us. He fully expects us to "take on" the whole wide world! And He has given us a Plan by which we can do it! Christian, is it your intention to impact *all nations* by "*turning men into disciples?*" Nothing less than this gigantic assignment is our Master's command. World impact is our mission. *Our goal must be to inform and impact the entire world to the ends of the earth until the end of time.*

This third point in the Commission may well be the most important of all. It is from this point that the disciple-making motivation arises. I want to spend some extra space at this point in order to assure that we recognize the magnitude of the Commission in impacting the entire world. Dr. D. Martyn Lloyd-Jones said in his book, ***The Miracle of Grace***, "I would not hesitate to say that finally there is no more thorough test of our individual profession of faith than our attitude toward the missionary enterprise of the Church." I might add to the words of this spiritual giant that "the missionary enterprise of the Church" is not merely the dispatching of specially burdened believers to distant foreign countries. It begins in *each* believer's heart and is carried out by each believer becoming a world-conscious, world-consumed, world-visionary disciple of Jesus Christ and building other world-visionary, world-impacting reproducing disciples.

Is your personal vision a "God-big" vision? How far does your intent to impact reach? The measure of your effectiveness as a disciple of Christ may be seen in answer to these questions: How far does your influence reach? How large is your sphere of magnitude? Isaiah 54:2 says, "Enlarge the place of thy tent, and let them stretch forth the curtains of thine habitations: spare not, lengthen thy cords, and strengthen thy stakes." This verse provides a perfect motto verse for disciple-makers (all true disciples of Christ), and it calls for an unceasing enlargement of each believer's vision to impact the entire world.

Again I ask you to face the question: How large is your sphere of magnitude? Do you work under a *hat*-sized vision, with the Christian life largely beginning and ending for the sake of *your own* survival and reward? Or is your vision *umbrella*-big, taking in perhaps two people? Or *phone booth*-sized, covering at most three or four? Or *room*-sized, including a few friends? Or *house*-sized, accommodating maybe 25 or 50? Or *department store*-sized, incorporating several hundred? Or *mall*-sized, able to contain several thousand? Or *gymnasium*-sized, enlarged to tens of thousands? *Or* do you aspire to a *sky*-sized vision which would include *every human being on earth and all future generations to come?* Remember that the Commission entails a Jesus-sized, God-big vision, and we are to increasingly become like Christ, thus developing the very Character of God. We became "partakers of His Divine Nature" (II Peter 1:4) at our conversion, and the remainder of our lives is to be spent cooperating with the expansion of His Nature in us. "He must increase, but I must decrease" (John 3:30). A part of this enlargement necessarily means a growing identification with the Divine Obsession—informing and impacting every person on earth with the Message of the Glorious Gospel of Christ.

It is apparent even from a surface reading of the Gospels that Jesus was out to invade, inform, and impact the whole wide world. He might have said, "I am the light of Galilee," but He didn't. He said, "I am the light of the world" (John 8:12). He did not say, "I am the light of Baptists or Presbyterians or Methodists." He did not say, "I am the light of the well-bred or the well-read or the well-fed." He might have said, "God so loved the Jews," but He didn't. He said, "God so loved the world" (John 3:16). Jesus emphatically stressed again and again that no smaller an area, no smaller a populace, than that of the world was ever in His mind. He is the only spiritual light for every land and for every person in every land on earth.

It is said that the soldiers of Napoleon's army carried in their knapsacks a map of the world in the tri-colors of France. They were "convicts," "prisoners," "captives," "slaves" of the idea of taking the world for France. Christian brothers and sisters, our Sovereign Lord has placed the burning vision of the whole world before the eyes of His people and has asked each of them to let it burn its way into his heart. And this vision is to constantly occupy our thoughts, our plans, our dreams, our activities, as long as we live. Once the vision begins to possess us, we will realize that Jesus patterned a plan for us—you and I as individuals—to implement and fulfill the vision. This is what visionary disciple-making is all about! Is that big, or is that big?

Ponder this question with your heart. Did the Bible and Christianity originate in any of the fifty states of the United States? No, Christianity is an "import" to these United States. Jesus was not born in my block or my neighborhood. The Bible was not originally written in English. *We Christians in America are the result of Christian missionaries.* Are we committed to doing in other parts of the world what those missionaries did for us? If you were one of the lost ones in Asia, Africa, or Latin America, would you want someone to bring you the message of Light and Life? Surely we self-centered Christians and our introverted, institutional "survival churches" must earnestly repent and ask the compassion and forgiveness of our Lord, because we have tried to make Him our possession (like the Jews did) instead of allowing ourselves to be possessed by Him. And our repentance must be of such depth that it leads to the *correction* of this tragic "humanistic Christianity" (my term, itself a contradiction of terms).

John Oxenham, in his volume, ***Bees in Amber***, wrote:

I hear a clear voice calling, calling,
Calling out in the night,
O, you who live in the Light of Life,
Bring Us the Light!
We are bound in the chains of darkness,
Our eyes receive no sight,
O, you who have never been bond or blind,
Bring us the Light!
You cannot—you shall not forget us,
Out here in the darkest night,
We are drowning men, we are dying men,
Bring, O bring us the Light!

Now, Christian, don't pull theology or proof-texts on me and tell me that men without God are dead and cannot talk like that! I know that. Believe me, I know that! This is not the way Godless men live, think, or speak—but it is the way every believer must think! We can't describe death to dead people, nor can we expect living impulses, activities, and speech from them. *Nor can we expect them to arise from the dead without hearing the voice that raises the dead!* Romans 10 makes it quite clear: no *proclamation* to lost people without *sent-ones* to proclaim the message, no *hearing* without such *proclamation*, no *faith* without *hearing*, and no *salvation* without *faith* (Romans 10:12-17)! Where does it begin in practical reality? With the sending and the saying! Is your church in the sending business? Is it spending to send so the message can be spoken? *The only alternative is radical disobedience to the command of the King of Kings and Lord of Lords.* What will our feeling and thinking be at the Judgment Seat of Christ if we spent our ministries focusing on the "Killer Bees"— buildings, budgets, bodies, bulletins, boasts, etc.?

Shortly before the middle of the last century, Charles Kingsley visited the New Hebrides Islands in the South Pacific Ocean and was appalled by the savagery and cannibalism existing there. On his return to Britain he wrote a pointed article declaring that the British government would render a service to the human race if it would send a war vessel to blast the natives into the sea like pestilential flies, because they were subhuman and nothing could ever be done to elevate them.

However, there were others who necessarily disagreed with Kingsley's assessment. Among them was a devoted Christian named John Paton of Dumfries, Scotland. Paton believed that the Gospel of Jesus is the power of God unto salvation (Romans 1:16), and that the Gospel has a quickening power to raise those dead in sin (Ephesians 2:1). After long journeying Paton reached the island of Tana in the New Hebrides, and in constant peril of his life preached Christ to these benighted people. I would invite any doubting reader to research the result for himself. When Paton died, the natives themselves erected a tombstone over his grave on which was inscribed this epitaph: "When he came, there was no light. When he died, there was no darkness." Today, dear friends, we can easily penetrate most of the earth at moderate cost and with little travel difficulty. We are "sitting" on vast resources which could be used to evangelize and disciple vast hordes of people over the world. Thousands of Christians, churches, and lost people would welcome and respond to our love in lands near and far; and we often sit in self-occupied disillusionment in dead and dying churches here in America. "Where there is no vision, the people perish."

On the very day that Pearl Harbor was attacked by Japanese bombers, a returned missionary from the Orient was met by a cynical acquaintance who, with a leer in his eye and a jeer in his voice, said, "Well, what do you think of your Japanese now?" To which the missionary quietly but confidently replied, as with the thrust of a sword, "*My* Japanese are very well, thank you, resting in the grace of God. If you are talking about the ones that just bombed the American fleet, those are *your* Japanese—the ones *you* were responsible for, but did nothing about. *They* are the ones causing the trouble. But *my* Japanese are doing quite well, thank you, trusting in the Lord Jesus Christ." Friends, what about "our" Brazilians, our Chileans, our Hondurans, our Guatemalans? What about our Filipinos, our Indonesians, our Mongolians, our Chinese, our New Guineans, our Yugoslavians, our Iraqis? Frank Laubach said, "If Americans had spent as much money on missions in Japan prior to World War II as we spent in building *one battleship* that was sunk at Pearl Harbor, we would likely never have had to fight that war to begin with." Are *you* involved in any real way in *world* impact? Are you *going* as a *sent-one* to make Christ known? If not, why not?

William James, the Harvard psychologist, wrote of a house in Chocorua, New Hampshire, as a young boy, "Oh, it's the most delightful house you ever saw. It has fourteen doors, all opening outwards." The very safety code that civic regulations impose upon our church buildings, that the church doors open outward for safety's sake, bespeak volumes of wisdom to us. A Christian, a church, a consuming vision, that operates with all doors opening outwards is a "delightful" thing, but frankly, the introverted Christian, the introverted church, should be eaten alive with his (its) own despair, disillusionment, frustration, and defeat!

Our world has been shrinking in size like a balloon as the air is let out. The airplane makes it possible for a person to fly in the rising sun from London to New York. I never travel overseas without meeting numbers of world-circling travelers. A voice captured by radio is heard on the opposite side of the earth sooner than it is heard in the rear of the auditorium where the words are spoken. A scene filmed for television is viewed in distant places exactly at the time of its occurrence. We live in the front yard (the living room?) of the world. The whole world has become one small neighborhood. What are we doing about our neighbors?

I look back over my last pastorate of ten years and try to remember the ways we sought to create world vision and world impact among the members of the Body:

(1) We used a "save your change" plan. Each member was encouraged to empty his pockets at the end of each day and put aside for missions all loose change except one coin of each denomination—a penny, nickel, dime, quarter, and half dollar. In December, we had a "missions march" in which we placed all these offerings before the Lord for His multiplication to the ends of the earth.

(2) We used a "Dollar-a-Week-For-Missions" plan. We asked each member to give an extra dollar a week (what American would miss that?) to world missions.

(3) We used the "functional Missions Committee" plan. We appointed the members with the most dominant world missionary spirit and vision, and asked them to "hold the world in front of us" constantly. We devoted quarterly services to a missions focus—with missionary speakers (including missionary wives and children), the reading of missionary letters, special prayer for "our" missionaries, etc.

(4) We used the "missionary home" plan. We owned two homes in which we regularly housed furloughing missionaries, and asked them to "traffic" our church with their information and influence.

(5) We used the "research our world" plan. We asked for geographical, political, economic, etc., informational reports about the many nations of the world. We especially tried to study the "ripe" areas, that is, the areas most responsive to the Gospel .

As an example, we employed such rationale as this. Suppose you owned a fruit orchard. In Field A, a worker would harvest five bushels an hour. In Field B, it would take five hours to harvest just one bushel. In Field C, nothing could be harvested because the fruit is still green. If you had thirty workers today, where would you send them? I think I would send twenty-nine of them to Field A so as not to lose the fruit there. I would send the other one to do what could be done in Field B and also to keep an eye on Field C. The job description for that one would be to let me know when those fields were ripe so I could reassign the personnel. Jesus called Himself "the Lord of the harvest" (Matthew 9:38). Has He mismanaged His business? Certainly not, but typically, His workers have not been listening to Him. Have YOU been praying the Lord of the harvest that He would "thrust forth laborers into His harvest"? Remember, "The field is the world" (Matthew 13:38).

(6) We used the "send a missionary" plan. How could I as a pastor ever be satisfied if God were not calling young people from the church I serve or my sphere of influence to mission stations over the world? I would certainly hold my ministry in suspicion. Just last week, we had a guest in our home who is between stops in the Orient (in a "closed" country), back in the United States only long enough to enlist more support and to bolster his teaching skills so he can be an "informal, amateur missionary" (that's a laugh; the vision dominates him!) in that dark land. Over a year ago now, he was instrumental in winning a young man to Christ, and discipling him, and already, that young man has won ten others to Christ! In a "closed" country! This "missionary" graduated from college with an electrical engineering degree, then returned to college after four years in the military to learn computer science so that he could get a teaching position in a university in the Oriental country. As I write these words, he is back in the states, sharpening his computer data and skills in order to be better equipped as a college teacher. Why? Because he has captured a vision for disciple-making that impacts the world. He told me again of his pilgrimage through (and appreciation for) the disciple-making process and the world-vision contagion of the church I was privileged to serve as pastor.

(7) We used the "dispatch temporary missionaries" plan. The world is open now to brief missions penetrations by small teams of people from churches in the states. The Southern Baptist International Mission Board is one mission agency

among many which offer short trips overseas to anyone for the sake of evangelism and world impact. The door to the world stands ajar. A steady stream of growing, happy, motivated, impacting Christians should be filing through it to the very ends of the earth. Some "mega-churches" should be sending at least 1,000 people per year to world-girdling mission projects. I have personally been on over one hundred major missions trips while continuing a very busy schedule at home. Just this week, a layman visiting in our city said to me, "I would be afraid to go to any country outside the United States." Afraid? That really should not occupy the mind of any Christian (read II Corinthians 11:23-33, and see how much fear dominated the docket of the Apostle Paul). Sadly, my friend was only confessing to me the failure of his church to infect him with Christ's Commission.

(8) We used the "study world religions" plan. This is self-explanatory, and included, when possible, testimonies from converts out of other world religions.

(9) We used the "profile missions" plan. When the Great Commission explodes upon the mind of a pastor as the dynamic of the Gospel, he will inevitably communicate his obsession in every situation. He will study the relationship of every major doctrine to this plan. He will "bleed" this passion through every sermon and presentation of the Gospel. He will expose his people to the missionary commitment of visionary believers. He himself will go to as many mission fields as possible, and take as many of his fellow Christians as possible with him.

Christian, are you "dreaming dreams" and "seeing visions" about world impact? "Ta ethne"—all ethnic groups, all nations—across the street and across the world. Has God hit you with an "Atlas Attack"—so that you "carry" the world for His sake? Are you pursuing the Savior's strategy, or have you succumbed to Satan's subtle substitute?

"Summit III," a conference on the Person of Christ and His redemptive work, was held in Chicago in December of 1986. Dr. Ralph Winter, General Director of the U.S. Center For World Mission, was in attendance. He was one of two people asked to respond at the end of the conference to the theme and its presentation. In his response, Dr. Winter called attention to the fact that the presentation had made no reference to the work of Christians and the Church in bearing witness of Christ and His work to the world. In short, the responsibility of believers for world-witness was not even mentioned.

When Dr. Winter completed his response, the chairman of the session, himself an outstanding and renowned Christian scholar, looked at Dr. Winter with a wry smile and said, "Well, we should have known that you would refer to your hobby sooner or later." Is world impact to be the *hobby* of a few fanatical enthusiasts, or is it to be the *heartbeat* of every—EVERY—Christian? *Can we truly affirm the Lordship of Jesus Christ and at the same time ignore the only mandate He ever gave to us as our marching orders?* Furthermore, could any group of Christians accurately or adequately discuss the Person and Work of Christ without specifying His focus on the world? It is incumbent upon us to ponder these questions all the way through to a satisfactory conclusion. The truth is that *every Christian should be a world Christian.* He should be committed to infecting others, interceding for missionaries, mission fields, and other Christians, invading the world, ingesting information, and thus inviting God to maximize his life for world impact.

Friends, our world is on fire—ablaze with change, turmoil, distress, revolution, violence, war—all the perfect raw materials for the Gospel. "Revolutions per minute" are occurring. "Is it nothing to you, all ye that pass by?"

One of the stories in Washington Irving's *Sketch Book* is the familiar story of a whimsical character named "Rip Van Winkle." Rip, you will remember, went into a 20-year sleep—to escape his own uselessness, boredom, and a vicious, bad-dispositioned wife. When he went to sleep, his home state of New York was one of the American colonies under English control and fighting the tyranny that oppressed the people there. But it wasn't the "larger tyranny" that bothered Rip; it was the smaller, local, self-centered, "practical" tyranny of an immediate bad home situation. By one long sleep, Rip was delivered from both tyrannies. Christian, are you listening? Rip's story is subtly symbolic. Pastors suffer from small, local tyrannies, and often duck into a chloroformed sleep (no vision, no dynamic, no world impact)—and they aren't even aware of the cosmic tyranny, Satan's strong grip on the whole world (I John 5:19b). So what happened in the story? Rip went soundly to sleep, and didn't awaken for twenty years. Meanwhile, a Revolutionary War was fought. When Rip went to sleep, he was ruled by George the Third of England—a king. When awakened, he lived in a democratic republic, and another George—General George Washington—was soon to assume leadership. Rip Van Winkle had *closed his eyes and slept right through a revolution!* Christian, are you listening? One cannot possibly know what he is missing when he is asleep. No wonder Satan wants you introverted—to your own guilt, your own prayers, your own Bible reading, your own faith, your own witness, your own faithfulness, your own ministry, your own church, your own sins, your own fears—a humanistic, survival brand of Christianity. Wake up,

Christian, and look at your Savior, look at your Bible, *look at your world, look at your opportunity* through new eyes!

Satan's Substitute

Meanwhile, back at Matthew 28:18-20, point three of the Commission! We have been looking extensively at the Savior's strategy under the heading, "Enlarge Your Vision." Now, let's momentarily look at Satan's substitute at this point. Satan is constantly turning our attention back to our own struggles, our own survival, the local institution in which we serve (and its success), etc. He is constantly seeking to shrink our vision to something traditional, institutional, or personal, and thus the overwhelming masses of the world's population never even hear of Christ and the Gospel. Jesus gave us a plan to impact the entire world, but we settle for a frustrating, disillusioning, non-productive substitute. Which plan are you following, the Savior's strategy by which you—yes, YOU—can actually impact the world, or Satan's substitute which secures the constant reduction of the Christian community and guarantees that billions will perish uninformed?

4. EVANGELIZE THE PROSPECTS

The fourth point of the Great Commission is to *Evangelize the Prospects.* There are seven verb forms in the Great Commission, but the only command (the only imperative mood verb) is to "turn men into disciples." In fact, the only imperative verb form (a command) in the entire paragraph (Matthew 28:16-20) is this verb: "turn men into disciples." This "evangelism" is a particular kind of evangelism, not to get "decisions for Christ," but rather to get "disciples" who will revolutionize the world.

The Savior's Strategy

Think carefully about this: since this is a command of Jesus—His *only* Marching Orders to His Church—it is impossible to truly *be* a disciple unless you are *making* disciples—*on his terms and by his strategy.* The "make disciples" clause is not an *addition* to Jesus' plan, but the very command itself. The issue is not "converts," but "disciples." So the Savior's strategy at this point is not merely soul-winning, but disciple-making. This means that what Jesus had done for His immediate disciples, He commanded them to do for others. They were to practice the same strategy, the same disciplines, and the same process, on others, that Jesus had used on them. My dear friend, please read this entire paragraph slowly, carefully, and prayerfully several times before proceeding further. We will examine the word "disciple" more extensively in a later study.

Satan's Substitute

What is Satan's substitute for making disciples? One part of his plan is to keep lost people lost, or to keep them from being saved. A second part is to keep believers from being world-visionary, world-impacting disciples. Or, if believers become disciples, Satan's purpose is to make them disciples of a pet idea, or a pet procedure; anything to keep them from being true, Christlike, New Testament disciples.

5. ENLIST THE EVANGELIZED

The fifth point of the Commission is to *Enlist the Evangelized.* "Baptizing them in the name of the Father, of the Son, and of the Holy Ghost."

The Savior's Strategy

The Savior's strategy for each believer is an identification with Jesus Christ that reveals death to everything the believer previously lived for, and a resurrection that means that he now lives only unto Christ. By baptism, a believer in Christ acknowledges death to his past—his past sins, his past selfishness, his past motivation, his past lifestyle, his past thought patterns—his entire past, and acknowledges that he now has only one real focus for living—the glorious Person and all-consuming Purpose of Jesus Christ. Baptism is a descent into a watery grave, a picture of entering into Christ's death, and a rising again from that grave, a picture of participation with Christ in His resurrection. So baptism reveals the believer's full enlistment and total involvement in Christian discipleship. The fact that it is "in the Name of the Father, and of the Son, and of the Holy Ghost" means that the believer is implicated in total involvement in the total Person and total Plan of God. Nothing in one's life is to be retained for his own purposes. Death has erased that possibility. Resurrection has secured another direction altogether for his life. Now, every resource of personality is devoted to the Lord Jesus Christ.

Satan's Substitute

What is Satan's substitute at this point of the Commission? Satan seeks to push the minds of men to two extremes. On the one hand, he says that baptism is a material, mechanical, ritualistic exercise, and thus it has no importance at all. So Quakers don't baptize at all—for that reason. On the other hand, Satan says that baptism is *all*-important and that sinners cannot have eternal life without it. So Campbellites make baptism the great capstone of eternal salvation. In the middle, holding the extremely weak view that baptism is a "mere symbol," are Southern Baptists and other church bodies.

A man came to work one day with two black eyes and a bruised and swollen face. A fellow workman asked, "What happened to you?" "My wife beat me up," was the meek reply. "Do you mean you let a mere woman do that to you?" His answer was, "Listen! There is nothing 'mere' about by wife!" Friends, when we say that any commission of Jesus involves a "*mere* picture," are we not on the side of Satan's substitute? Nothing Jesus ever *said* is "mere"! Have you seen how big your enlistment by Jesus Christ and your involvement with Jesus Christ really are?

6. EDUCATE AND EDIFY THE ENLISTED

The sixth point of the Great Commission is to *Educate and Edify* all the enlisted. "Teaching them to observe (obey) all things whatsoever I have commanded you." Again, the lead verb is a present participle. It indicates an ongoing, unceasing, uninterrupted, continual activity.

The Savior's Strategy

There is never to be a moment of my life as a Christian when I am not teaching! Whether by intentional example, overt statement, specific planned curriculum, silent influence, structured or unstructured settings, I am to be an indefatigable communicator of the One Who is my Life. Every believer is to be a teacher, whether he has the gift of teaching or not. The means of communication which are available today are so many and so convincing that a Christian can hardly offer a valid excuse for not teaching. Cassette tapes on every conceivable Christian subject and produced by

Godly, skilled Christian communicators; video tapes of top quality and content; vast libraries of books which may be obtained by loan or purchase; regular publications which contain a variety of teaching articles and studies, etc., etc. Every Christian's residence should be a repository and a circulation station for these teaching means. Every Christian Church should be a disseminating station for Gospel truth, using every available means and every available member to penetrate hearts, homes, community establishments, etc., with the total truth of the Gospel. Each Christian should be a special target for endless discipleship and disciple-making teaching. World vision and world ministries should be dynamically kept before each Christian and each church. The goal? That every Christian and every church have on his (its) heart what God has on His: the impacting of the entire world by building and deploying world-visionary, world-impacting Christians.

Satan's Substitute

What is Satan's substitute at this point? He first seeks to prevent the anointed teaching of the great truths of the Bible at all. Then he seeks to make "sermon-tasters" out of Christians. In this manner, they will be immunized from true Christianity by a mild inoculation of the real thing. Or he makes believers into analysts or sifters of truth, presuming that they can discern and appreciate truth apart from the Holy Spirit. Thus, they assume superiority over the truth and over the teacher of the truth. The New Testament word for "obedience," *hupokonan*, means "to hear under," and it pictures a person listening to God's truth from a consistent position of humility. James M. Barrie said, "Life is one long lesson in humility," and this is certainly true of the Christian life. But Satan's strategy is to cancel this possibility of humble listening to truth, and thus to turn the believer back into a self-governed, self-centered life-style.

Satan's plan for the believer is evident to a perceptive, sensitive Christian. Let me employ a word that shows the end result of Satan's plan. It is the word "reprobate." To "bate" means to "suspend." The prefix "pro" means "before" or "in front of." To "probate," then, is to suspend in front of. When this action is repeated, this is called "re-probating," or repeated probating. It is Satan's delight when a believer parades to church Sunday after Sunday and allows the truth to pass freely in front of him. The first time he does this without humble reception of that truth into the broken soil of a humble, sensitive, obedient heart, he "probates" that truth. The second time he does it, he "reprobates" that truth. It is quite easy to see that this is the weekly procedure of the average church member, Sunday by Sunday, week after week, month after month, year after year. He has become convinced that attending church and listening to the sermon IS the Christian life. When this procedure has continued until the person can actually no longer adjust to truth in the proper way by brokenness, humility, and prayerful obedience, God steps into the picture and turns the word "reprobate" back upon this regular listener. He becomes a lifeless, powerless, vision-less "pew potato" in a local church. He may or may not cause overt trouble for the church and the pastor, depending on the degree of his guilt over his diversion. You see, it was people who constantly went to church and constantly "handled" truth and constantly analyzed it who were guilty of the reprobate mind and the unpardonable sin. They were the scribes and Pharisees, the best and most religious people of their day (see Matthew 12). So Satan wants us to be "cafeteria line Christians," constantly appraising the truth, and picking and choosing with regard to our favorite truths, our favorite preachers, and our favorite sermons. Thus, point six in the Great Commission is neutralized by Satan's substitute strategy.

Christian, on which side do you fall? Are you pursuing the Savior's strategy with all the humble industry of your spirit, or are you "trampling God's courts" as a regular auditor who is completely non-productive in fulfilling the Great Commission?

7. EXPECT HIM TO WORK

Point seven of the Great Commission is to *Expect Jesus Christ To Work.* "And lo, I am with you all the days, even to the end of the age." Please note that the "lo" follows the "go." The promise of Christ's special Presence in this verse belongs only to those who are pouring their lives into all the prescribed activities to fulfill the Great Commission. In other words, you cannot validly claim the *promise* unless you follow the *plan.* We will never have New Testament *power* until we follow New Testament *patterns.* So most of our prayers for the Holy Spirit and His power are wasted prayers. What do we want that power for? Why do we seek His fullness? To secure God's approval on our plans? To enhance our reputations? To put a brand of success on our endeavors for Him? Remember God's answer to the great preacher's prayer: "My child, *with plans no bigger than yours, you don't need my power.*"

The Savior's Strategy

What is the Savior's strategy? It is to personally attend the efforts of every disciple-maker and anoint his life and activity with the great power of the Holy Spirit. Jesus said, "And lo, I *myself* (the word is very emphatic) am with you all the days, even to the end of the age." Every Christian is an inadequate, incapable, insufficient, powerless representative of Jesus Christ apart from this promise (actually, it is a *fact*, not a mere promise). But every amateur in any field knows what an encouragement, what an enablement it is to have the regular attending presence of *the expert* with him. What did Jesus mean when He said, "I Myself am with you?" He meant that the disciple-maker has the *actual* Presence of Jesus with him. The Holy Spirit may best be understood as Christ's "alter ego," or His "other self." He meant that the disciple-maker has the *abiding* Presence of Jesus with him. There is never a moment, never a situation, never a circumstance when the disciple-maker is living to fulfill the Commission when He is without the Presence of the Risen and Powerful Son of God. The day will never come when the Lord Jesus is not powerfully present in the life of His disciple-making saint. He meant that the disciple-maker has the *active* Presence of Jesus with him at all times. Jesus is not with us as an anonymous or silent or inactive partner. The last verse of the Gospel of Mark declares that "they went forth, and preached everywhere, *the Lord working with them*, and confirming the word with signs following" (Mark 16:20). The "signs" may be questionable and variable, but the Presence of Jesus is constant!

John Wesley White said, "To be filled with the 'holy go' is to be filled with the 'Holy Ghost.'" People often quote this promise out of its proper setting. When they are in adversity, they use this verse to claim that the Lord is always with them. But this verse isn't a balm for adversity. There are plenty of verses in Scripture which may be used for that purpose, but this isn't one of them—unless, of course, the adversity comes as a direct result of fulfilling the Commission. This is a verse for the disciple-maker. In other words, if you wonder where to find Jesus today, you must look where disciples are being made. He by-passes many a church where sermons are preached (and even *good* sermons), where prayers are prayed (and even *sincere* prayers), and where crowds gather (and they may even be *big* crowds), and goes to approve and anoint any person who is making disciples *according to his New Testament pattern.*

Do you want to know where Jesus will be attending church next Sunday? Look for Him in a church where world-visionary, world-impacting reproducers of world-visionary, world-impacting reproducers are being made. Not merely "good Christians," mind you, because that is usually merely a humanistic brand of Christianity. Jesus doesn't attend and anoint and approve many churches and many believer's lives because they don't have on their hearts what God has on His heart, to "turn men into disciples in all nations." On the other hand, when God sees a disciple-making church (building disciples after His pattern and fully depending upon Him in this gigantic undertaking), He gets thoroughly involved there. He gets down-right, in-right, up-right, out-right enthused and excited about it—and He joins that church right away. And He will meet with the people of that church as long as He can enjoy Himself there.

We need no bigger proof of the bigness of the Commission than to see the statements Jesus put before and after it. "All authority is given unto Me in heaven and on earth." "And lo, I Myself am with you all the days, even unto the very end of the age." "All the days"—in days of peril or days of safety, in days of failure and of success, of freedom or restriction, of peace or war, of sowing or reaping, of study or action. There will never be a day when this fact fails.

When Fretyof Nansen, the great Norwegian explorer, set sail in 1896 to penetrate the polar ice cap and study the flow of polar ice, everyone knew it was a hazardous undertaking. He took with him a cage of carrier pigeons. At each stage of the perilous journey, he released one of the birds with a message attached to its leg. Mrs. Nansen's journal at home contained this entry: "I was overjoyed each time I found one of the pigeons at my window. When I saw the bird, I knew my husband was alive and thinking of me." Two thousand years ago, the glorified Lord Jesus Christ released the Heavenly Dove, the Holy Spirit, His Other Self, into the world on the Day of Pentecost—the full release of Divine Power for the fulfillment of the Divine Plan. When we obey Him and see the working of His mighty Spirit, we know He is alive and well, thinking of us, and present and active with us. It is His desire and pleasure to act this way all the time. This is His strategy.

Satan's Substitute

What is Satan's subtle substitute? He tries to divert our attention to institution-building and other reduced activities, and thus preclude the involvement of the Holy Spirit with us. Or, he tries to convince us that we are all alone and that no one is listening when we pray. He tries to keep us ignorant of the Holy Spirit or indifferent to His Person, Presence, and power, or occupied with a self-centered counterfeit experience of Him.

On which side, dear Christian, do you fall at this point? The Great Commission or the Great Omission?

We have examined the Commission that determines our mandate. Remember, it is the only marching orders Jesus ever gave to His church. However, Satan keeps the Divine Plan hindered by keeping his own program in operation. Wherever the church is DIVERTED to institution-building, or self-survival, or merely making "good Christians," Satan's hand is evident. In that case, the Great Commission has become the "Great Omission." Isn't it time that we put the "see" back into the Commission?

Years ago, I taught this study on the Great Commission in a group of young married couples. At the conclusion of the session, a young housewife prayed this prayer which I copied from a cassette tape later:

Father, I glory in the fact that there is a man, a human being, in heaven for us right now. And if He IS and REMAINS truly human, then He must still have human emotions. He can enjoy, appreciate, hurt, and suffer. HOW HIS HEART MUST GRIEVE as He seeks to administrate His cause on earth, but watches His earthly Body following a strategy that is generally the EXACT OPPOSITE at every point to that strategy which He gave to His disciples.

Great Commission or Great Omission? Friends, isn't it time that we put the "see" back into the Great Commission?

Chapter 3
The Concept that Determines Our Method

"Turn men into disciples . . ." Matthew 28:19

If we are to be thoroughly obedient to Jesus Christ and His Great Commission, we must force ourselves to be technically accurate in understanding that Commission. We cannot afford ourselves the indulgence of ignorance or inaccuracy. We live "by every word that proceeds out of the mouth of God," and nowhere is that declaration more binding than with regard to the Great Commission. Since the only command in the Commission is to "turn men into disciples," it is incumbent upon us to know our job description as fully as we can know it. Once we have learned that the only command in the Great Commission is to "turn people into disciples," several crucial questions should be asked. The first is, What is a disciple? The second is, What does it mean to turn people into disciples? And the third is, How do we do it? I cannot imagine any questions that are more important for today's church, else we continue to ignorantly follow "Satan's subtle substitute" instead of obeying the Savior's strategy.

We have seen how vital vision is to spiritual function, and we have examined the Great Commission, the commission which determines our Mandate. Now, we will investigate the concept that determines our method. The concept is that of disciple-making. In order to understand the concept fully, we need to explore a family of related words, some of which are actually used in the Bible, and some of which are "coined" from the Biblical words and their use.

DISCIPLE-MAKING

The concept that determines our method is that of discipleship: "Turn men into disciples," Jesus commanded. Several key words call for our best attention.

DISCIPLE

One is the word "disciple." "Disciples are both the people who please the Lord and the people who will reach the world. Therefore, a clear identification of a disciple is imperative. Understanding what a disciple is and what a disciple does are top priorities for the church. The irony of the church is that we throw the word 'disciple' around freely, but too often with no definition. Such a condition is like a shoe company trying to produce a product without specifications. The product coming off the end of the assembly line would be interesting." (Bill Hull; ***The Disciple Making Pastor***, 54).

This word, "disciple," has been tragically reduced in the modern church, including everything from "convert" to "professing believer." Usually, "making disciples" is defined by "winning people to Christ." Soul-winning is a vital part, a beginning part, a necessary part, of disciple-making, but it is only a beginning. If the process stops with soul-winning, the sinner in question is not really "won" at all.

In the New Testament, the word is employed in several general ways, then in an increasingly narrow way. It is used, first, to describe a *casual listener.* All of those who came to hear Jesus at the beginning of His ministry are called "disciples." Then, it is used to describe a *convinced listener*, a person who consents that what he is hearing is true, though it may not substantially change his life or his lifestyle. Read John 6 carefully, giving special attention to verses 63-66. The casual and convinced listeners, while still uncommitted followers, left Jesus and "walked no more with Him." Friends, the church today is full of people who meet these two descriptions. This comprises the vast congregation of "pew potatoes" who fill our churches Sunday after Sunday, but who have no power with God in changing the world, because they are not truly and deeply changed themselves.

The third use of the word "disciple" in the New Testament defines a *committed, lifelong learner and follower.* This last use is the one Jesus intended in the Great Commission, and it constitutes our marching orders. We are to go everywhere and "turn men into *committed, lifelong learners and followers* of Jesus Christ." You see, this meaning is inherent in the word "disciple." A disciple is an *adherent* (one who adheres, like adhesive tape, to another), or an *apprentice*, of Jesus Christ. Weigh each definitive word carefully. Indeed, spend some time exploring the words. A disciple is a *person in training.* Indeed, he is a leader in training.

Tertullian, one of the leaders of the early church, called Christians "pupils in God's school." A disciple is first born, then he is made. He is born by the Spirit of God with the right factory-installed equipment. But, then he must be built, trained, taught, and led to commitment to Jesus Christ.

Waldron Scott, a great disciple-maker, wrote: "The very activity of developing new attitudes, acquiring new skills, formulating new relationships, discovering, daring, exploring, reforming, renewing—in short, learning—makes life the adventure Jesus promises it will be. If you're not learning, you're not living. It's as pure and simple as that."

However, even with such a quality statement, and by such a quality man, we must be gravely cautious. One dimension needs to be emphatically added to Scott's statement: t*he focus of the learning and living is to be Jesus Christ, and the outcome is to be practical likeness to Jesus Christ.* A New Testament disciple is completely preoccupied with Jesus Christ so that this preoccupation consumes all lesser possibilities; and he is, thus, becoming more and more like Christ in a practical way—constantly *teaching*, constantly *ministering*, constantly *building people's lives*, constantly *correcting* where necessary, and constantly *going after the whole wide world*!

So, practical Christ-likeness is not the meek-mannered, timid, tame, insipid sentiment that we have thoughtlessly allowed in today's church. Eugenia Price was within range of a great truth when she said, "The greatest sin of today's church is that it has tamed Jesus Christ." Sam Shoemaker, about whom Billy Graham said, "He probably meant more to the institutional church world-wide than any man of his generation," once wrote: "It is not the main job of the church to turn out a lot of work, list a long string of members, or raise a lot of money. It is the main job of the church to fashion people who behave like Jesus Christ—and that is not a mild lifestyle, nor is it a way people don't act. These Christ-like people cannot be hewn out of the mediocre mass wholesale, but only one by one."

Contrast our churches and their strategy today, in which the procedure is something like blowing up a mountain of granite and expecting to get a number of polished statues. Shoemaker continued: "Our churches should be stripped down to miniature organizations and thus afford pastors and laymen the opportunity to learn the great spiritual art of winning and training others. It seems an almost universal experience that unless one puts this kind of work first in his life, it will be crowded out entirely. Our minds, our emotions, the hours of our days, should be filled with a special group of individuals at all times—individuals we seek to win, individuals we seek to train in taking responsibility, individuals to whom we ourselves look for spiritual fellowship and help." This lifestyle was, of course, originally modeled by Jesus, and it should be mastered by us, also.

Knofel Staton wrote insightfully and incisively when he said, "Who is a disciple of Jesus and how do we make one? Without a clear picture of our objectives we will spin our wheels, use up our time and energy, and still not make any disciples." The word "disciple" is used 270 times in the Gospels and in the Book of Acts. The word does not occur again in the remaining 22 books of the New Testament. What is going on here? Why does the word disappear? What is the Holy Spirit saying? In Luke 6:40, Jesus said, "When the process is completed, the pupil will be like his teacher." So, we should expect some terms to emerge which picture advancing likeness. And, indeed, the word "Christian" begins to be used. The word "saint"—one completely set aside to Christ's control—begins to emerge. The word "believer"—one who is a continued and consistent believer in Jesus Christ, cleaving to Him and pursuing His purposes in his own practical daily life—is often used.

DISCIPLER

A second key word is the word "discipler." A discipler, or disciple-maker, is a person who "turns men into disciples." A discipler is merely a maturing disciple, for one surely cannot be a disciple of Jesus while ignoring the only marching orders Jesus gave to His church. In short, it would seem to be impossible to be a disciple without being a discipler. A discipler is a co-learner who recruits and leads others as they are learning together.

DISCIPLING

A third key word is the word "discipling." The command of Jesus to "make disciples" is loaded with implications based on Jesus' example and teaching. Discipling is the process of building men into disciples. Christopher Adsit, in his book *Personal Disciple-Making*, defines it as "seeking to fulfill the imperative of the Great Commission by making a conscientious effort to help people move toward spiritual maturity—drawing on the power and direction of the Holy Spirit, utilizing the resources of the local church, and fully employing the gifts, talents, and skills acquired over the years."

Discipling is done by *someone, not by something.* It is done by *persons, not by programs.* It is accomplished by *individuals, not by institutions.* Technically, discipling is one Christian person imparting his whole life to another, by example, leadership, and relationship. It always involves life transference.

There is a great deal of difference between *disinfecting sinners* and *discipling saints.* Most church work—pastoral work, worship, educational efforts, promotional efforts, etc.—results in the occasional disinfecting of sinners, but there is pitifully little true discipling of saints. Proof of the point? Very simply, most Christians in most churches have no more "spiritual clout" for Christ than they did the day before they were saved!

Disinfecting of sinners gets the sinner saved, then puts him in a spiritual safety deposit box from which he emerges as a tamed and decent human being. Discipling of saints, on the other hand, involves the qualitative construction of a saved individual so that individual will *change the world* in an ever-enlarging way by continuing the process.

The difference may be seen in this illustration. It involves a comparison between preaching and disciple-making. Suppose you have a person standing behind a line, holding a bucket of water in his hand. Twenty feet beyond the line, there are 20 small-mouth milk bottles. Preaching is like throwing the water out of the bucket from behind the line, hoping that some of the water enters the bottles. However, the efficiency of such a technique is fairly predictable: not much water will get into the bottles. And even if it does, it will evaporate in time if there is not a practical purpose for its use. Disciple-making, by comparison, is like taking the bucket of water to each milk bottle and pouring the water into it until the bottle is full. There is little question where the greater efficiency lies.

Or, preaching is like holding an eyedropper of medicine out a third-story window and dispensing it onto the street below, hoping some of it will hit somebody in the eye. Disciple-making, on the other hand, is personal, close-up application, like dispensing the medicine from the tip of the eyedropper directly into the needy eye.

Without a constant standard of discipling, we dispense the truth in a mass way and *count the people*—though we may be producing *very few people who count.* Discipling in a style like that of Jesus will correct that problem. When the disciples heard Jesus say that they were to "turn men into disciples," they had to interpret that to mean that they were to make out of others what Jesus had made out of them. Discipling includes the entire disciple-making process, from conversion to trained disciple-maker. This is the very heart of what Christ expects of His church.

DISCIPLINES

A final key word is the word "disciplines." Disciplines are the areas of life that reveal the cost of discipleship. Hudson Taylor, the founder of the China Island Mission and one of the greatest visionary missionary-statesmen who has ever lived, wrote: "A man may be consecrated, dedicated and devoted, but of little value if undisciplined."

How serious is Christ's mandate? How extensive and serious is the church's failure to obey the one command of the Commission? Is there real evidence of such failure? I believe the evidence is prevailing and pervasive.

I was in a meeting years ago with a veteran, white-haired Christian who has long ago gone to Heaven. He and I were alone in his office for awhile, at which time he asked me what I was "doing these days" in the church of which I was pastor. I replied, "I'm doing everything I know to do to turn church members into world-visionary disciples who are, in turn, reproducers of other world-visionary disciples." He sadly replied to me, "Brother Hodges, I never had any success producing reproducers in any church where I was pastor." I asked, "Then what did you do?" He sadly replied, "I just went ahead and tried to do all the work myself." I cannot imagine a sadder self-judgment!

I was seated in a restaurant with three pastors as we were waiting for lunch to be served. We were talking (I suppose at my lead) about disciple-making. One fine pastor in the group made an honest assessment of his ministerial history (and he was a fine, leading evangelical pastor): "Herb, I look back over two long pastorates and I can only see two men in each of the two churches who might qualify as the kind of men you are defining." He was not in protest or in anger when he spoke, only sadness. How tragic, but how typical! At best, we have been producing "good Christians," which often means extremely introverted people, instead of world-impacting, reproducing disciple-makers.

The apparent goal of Jesus was to produce "disciples" who would become "disciplers," engaged in a lifetime vocation of "discipling" others and practicing the daily "disciplines" which are necessary to fulfill that purpose.

DISCIPLE-MAKING THAT PRODUCES A MINISTRY OF MULTIPLICATION

Then, the New Testament adds another crucial dimension to our vocation. We are to be engaged in discipleship *that produces a ministry of multiplication.* It was clearly Christ's intent that each disciple be engaged in a multiplying ministry. What is multiplication? Multiplication is when disciplers start producing other visionary, world-impacting disciplers. You see, God's plan is to *reach* the world exactly the same way it was *populated—by multiplication.* In Genesis 9:1,

God said, "Be fruitful, and multiply, and replenish the earth." Someone said this was the first order ever given to man, and the only one he has obeyed. Jesus' evangelistic mandate is essentially the same as God's biological mandate.

Why do men fail to multiply biologically?

1. Some never marry, or there is no union of the sexes. Thus, multiplication does not occur.

2. Some suffer from disease or impairment to some vital reproductive part of the body.

3. Some don't multiply because of immaturity. You simply don't know any three-year-old fathers! The reproductive organs are present, but they are not sufficiently developed to allow reproduction. Babies don't reproduce.

The same deficiencies account for the failure to multiply spiritually. When there is no union between a Christian and Jesus Christ on a consistent basis, there will be little or no spiritual multiplication. The presence of sin in a believer's life will also impede the process of multiplication. In addition, the stalemating of a Christian in spiritual babyhood will prevent multiplication. Paul said, "I wrote unto you as unto babes in Christ," and the baby Christians in Corinth missed the world-impacting standard of spiritual multiplication.

Spiritual multiplication is God's planned vision for reaching our present world and all future generations through those we win and train now. The strategy of Jesus' ministry was evident: He looked at the masses through the man, then He built the man to impact the masses. He ministered to everyone before Him—but He only recruited for His

Kingdom's sake. How we have distorted these standards in building institutions instead of individuals. Jesus loved each individual, to be sure, but He always looked beyond His disciples to the men they would reach and train (see John 17:20).

In Acts 2:41, 47 and Acts 5:14, the word "added" defines God's mathematical strategy at the very beginning of church history. However, in Acts 6:1, we read that "the number of the disciples was multiplied greatly so that a great company of priests was added unto the faith." Then, by Acts 9:31, we read that "the churches . . . were multiplied." Apparently, the church never returned to mere additions unless it went out on the frontier and had to begin all over again, and even then it quickly moved back to multiplication.

When a person my age is reunited with a college or seminary classmate whom he hasn't seen since school days, several key questions are usually asked. "Are you married?" "Do you have any children?" "How many children?" "Do you have any grandchildren?" And, if the persons are old enough, they ask, "Do you have any great-grandchildren?"

When we stand at the Judgment Seat of Christ, we may well hear these same questions. "Do you have any children (and if not, why not)?" "How many children?" Then the real test of our participation in Jesus' plan begins. "Do you have any grandchildren, people who are Christians because of the way you built your own spiritual children?" "And, do you have any spiritual great-grandchildren?" It will not be satisfying to know that we ministered to vast numbers and a few became producers. It will only be satisfying if we have spent our lives seeking to make out of our disciples *what Jesus made out of His.*

In order to be sure we see the true standard and understand the seriousness of failure to follow it, let me conclude this chapter on a very serious, even negative, note. The well-known book, ***The Bridge Over the River Kwai***, was made into an even better-known movie by the same title. They were suggested by Ernest Gordon's excellent book, ***Miracle On the River Kwai***, although the book and movie about the bridge are fictional take-offs from the original.

The Bridge Over the River Kwai tells the story of a British colonel captured by the Japanese during World War II. In the concentration camp in a Burmese jungle, hundreds of hopeless prisoners languished near death. The English officer came up with a creative plan to improve morale and give the captives something to live for. Near the camp, the enemy was constructing a railroad bridge. The prisoners would take over the task. They would work with arrogant efficiency and show the Japanese what English ingenuity could do! Dedicating himself and his soldiers to the job, the British leader saw morale change. The goal of building the bridge became his magnificent obsession. Finally, the crossing was finished. As the first Japanese supply train chugged toward the structure, the proudly patrolling colonel spied Allied commandos in the river bed under the bridge, about to demolish the bridge. Because of his private obsession, he screamed to warn the Japanese commander and ran frantically down the river, trying to stop the saboteurs.

Isn't the analogy clear? Many churches languish near death, so their leaders come up with one plan after another, program upon program, to improve morale and give the members something to keep them motivated. In short, they engage in survival strategies, a classic example of institution-building. Just as in the story, the enemy has his own program, and he is happy to enlist us in its "fulfillment." We often take over his plan with a vengeance. The goal of "building the bridge" becomes our magnificent obsession. When anyone suggests that this is more of Satan's substitute than it is the Savior's strategy, we turn on him as if he were our enemy. So obsessed have we become with institution-building programs that we have forgotten that there is a battle bigger than the bridge going on. Like little children playing make-believe games, we skip breathlessly through life largely missing the original mandate of Jesus.

In the spring of 1991, I spent a week in a Texas church, preaching at night on themes that support the disciple-making process, and teaching in the noontime services the process itself. The pastor of this church emerged from the ministry of a church I had earlier served as pastor. On the final evening, a young married couple approached me moments before the service began, and as we talked, the wife placed a folded letter in my hand. In part, the letter said: "I don't know if you know it or not, but I am one of your spiritual grandchildren. Our pastor has been discipling me and my husband for about four years." Then there is a section of personal information and another section in which she rehearses and applies the message of each evening of that week. Then she writes:

Thank you for the extra time you've spent teaching us about discipleship. I'm afraid I'm a lot like the brother who confessed in tears in a noon service that he had been a Christian for a long time, but had never really discipled anyone. I've witnessed to several after learning and being with our pastor, but I'm now anxious for my first disciple to come into my life. This week has been a <u>turning point</u> in my life, and I appreciate you letting God use you to minister and challenge me. I plan, with Jesus working through me, to make you a spiritual great-grand-

father. Thank you so much for coming! Your sister and grand-child in Christ, (signature).

The practical New Testament realities suggested by the sentiment of that letter comprise the marching orders Jesus gave to His church. Add the dimensions of spiritual reproduction, world vision, and the practical process of making disciples, and you have made a giant stride toward the fulfillment of His mandate.

In May of 1983, a Southern Baptist seminary periodical carried a sad, even tragic, story. I will withhold the names of the persons involved, though they were recorded in the story. "When missionaries . . . wrote a book about being thrown out of Ethiopia, they were forced to ask themselves what they really left behind. The answer knocked the wind out of them. They realized that they had only scattered seeds, not planted them. Even more sobering was their realization that Christians everywhere were making the same mistake: baptizing multitudes, but not making disciples. 'We haven't made disciples,' the missionary told a chapel audience. 'We have simply had professions of faith. We have them sitting in pews all over America and around the world. It's fairly easy to baptize folks. It's a different ball game to make disciples. It seems to me that the church and God have two different plans of operation. The church has speakers and listeners, neither of which are the doers that Jesus calls Christians to be. We need to get in on God's program.'"

This account probably generalizes the problem as if all Christians were equally blameworthy, and it surely oversimplifies the solution. This book is also guilty of both faults. However, it does address a crucial failure in the church at large, and it does remind us of the one strategy Jesus gave.

It is never too late to begin doing what is right—what we have been commanded to do. Anyone can "go back to square one" and begin the multiplication process. However, most of us would need to give ourselves immediately to a vocation of studying the life and ministry of Jesus, asking, "How did He do it with His men?" and studying also the great works on the disciple-making, multiplying process. I would suggest beginning with Robert Coleman's ***Master Plan of Evangelism***, then Leroy Eims' ***The Lost Art of Disciple-Making.*** These need to be read over and over. From that point, the specialized works available today would occupy the most serious disciple-maker for the rest of his life.

I can envision a growing army of world-visionary, world-impacting, reproducing multipliers whose entire history is a commitment to Jesus' Commission to "turn men into disciples." May God recruit and deploy that army before our very eyes.

Chapter 4
The Key that Hangs at the Front Door of Church History

"The former treatise have I made, O Theophilus, of all that Jesus began both to do and teach, Until the day in which he was taken up, after that he through the Holy Ghost had given commandments unto the apostles whom he had chosen: To whom also he showed himself alive after his passion by many infallible proofs, being seen of them forty days, and speaking of the things pertaining to the kingdom of God: And, being assembled together with them, commanded them that they should not depart from Jerusalem, but wait for the promise of the Father, which, saith he, ye have heard of me. For John truly baptized with water; but ye shall be baptized with the Holy Ghost not many days hence." *Acts 1:1-5 KJV*

We will begin this study at the "front door" of "The Acts of the Apostles." Christian history has been marked by some debate about the title of this book in the Bible. You probably know that the names of the books in the New Testament are not inspired. They were added many years after the completion of the New Testament. Some believe this particular book should be called "The Acts of Some of the Apostles," because only the ministries of Peter, James, John and Paul are referred to. Others think it should be called "The Acts of the Holy Spirit" to highlight the Main Worker and hide the lesser workers. But, everyone retains the word "Acts" in the title. Note that it is not the intentions, or the plans, or the hopes, or the ambitions, or the studies, or the meditations, or the sermons (ouch!), of the Apostles. It is the *acts* of the apostles. If the apostles had stopped with any of the possibilities mentioned above, the book would never have been written. It is my prayer for us, as we open the front door of the book, that we will get "caught in the Acts"!

We will begin with an extended look at the very first verse. "The former treatise have I made, O Theophilus, of all that Jesus began both to do and teach." Let me impose an outline on the verse. First, there is a *previous document* mentioned here ("the former treatise"). Then, there is a *personal disciple* identified here ("O Theophilus"). Finally, there is a *plain declaration* of purpose for writing the previous document, and, by suggestion, a declaration of purpose for writing the present document.

PREVIOUS DOCUMENT MENTIONED

Let's think of the *previous document* that is mentioned here. What is that "former treatise"? The Phillips paraphrase calls it "my first book." The Amplified Bible translates it "the former account which I prepared." The previous document is, of course, the Gospel According to Luke. The Gospel According to Luke is one of the four Gospels in the New Testament. It is comprised of 24 chapters in your Bible, and is roughly constructed around some ten historical facts about the Person of Jesus Christ. The ten facts are: His Virgin Birth; His Sinless Life; His Baptism; His Temptation; His

Transfiguration; His Garden of Gethsemane Struggle; His Crucifixion and Death; His Burial; His Resurrection; and His Ascension.

To see how remarkable this is, note the first of these historical facts about Jesus, His virgin birth. Remind yourself that Luke was a medical doctor. Medical doctors don't easily believe in virgin births, but the most extensive account of Jesus' virgin birth in the entire Bible is given by Dr. Luke. He tells us in the first chapter of his Gospel that he had researched the historical data about Jesus perfectly, and that he wrote on the basis of his findings. So, we have another great evidence here for the integrity and authenticity of the story of Jesus Christ.

WHO WAS LUKE AND HOW DID HE GET INTO THE STORY?

Who was Luke? And how did he get into the Gospel story? He was a Gentile man—his name indicates this. He was a medical doctor called "Luke, the beloved physician" in Colossians 4:14. Sometimes we have the idea that everyone in the primitive world was backward, largely illiterate, and certainly not as enlightened as we are today. But such is hardly the case. Luke has been often challenged as an historian and as a medical doctor, but this anvil (Luke and his writings) has broken many a hammer (his critics). In fact, at every point of challenge, the writings of Luke have stood the test and won the day, both historically and medically.

Entire volumes have been written about Luke, both as an historian and as a medical doctor. For example, Dr. Hobart published a worthy volume entitled ***The Medical Language of Luke***, which concedes the brilliance and accuracy of Luke's technical use of medical terminology in both his books. As usual, when the sciences investigate objectively, they finally catch up with the Bible!

But, how did this medical doctor become involved in Gospel apologetics and the writing of two books which are in our New Testament? Let's combine history, revelation, and reason for a few moments. Paul and Silas came to the region of Galatia on Paul's second missionary journey (Acts 16:6). While they were there, Paul apparently contracted a very, very serious eye disease (or an earlier disease deteriorated to an extremely incapacitating level). When he wrote back to the Galatians later, he said, "You see how large a letter I have written unto you with mine own hand" (Galatians 6:11, KJV). Goodspeed translates, "See what large letters I make." Knox says, "Here is some bold lettering for you." The New English Bible renders it, "You see these big letters?" So, you see Paul straining with pen over parchment, blocking out gigantic letters because he cannot see well enough to write normally.

In Galatians 4:13-15, Paul said to them, "You know how through infirmity of the flesh I preached the Gospel unto you at the first. And my trial which was in my flesh ye despised not, nor rejected; but received me as an angel of God, even as Christ Jesus... for I bear you record, that if it had been possible, *ye would have plucked out your own eyes, and have given them to me.*" Note that God did not heal Paul of this serious defect. He had something much bigger and better in mind than the healing of His Apostle! He was about to recruit (through Paul's illness) one of His leading spokesmen!

Paul and his team pressed on from SE to NW in the "corridor" of Asia Minor until they came to the city of Troas, a seacoast town on the northern arm of the Aegean Sea. Paul may have had great difficulty sleeping peacefully, for it was here that "a vision appeared to Paul in the night; There stood a man of Macedonia, and prayed him, saying, Come over into Macedonia, and help us." Thus, the evangelization of Southern Europe was begun.

While Paul waited, puzzled, at Troas, he knew he needed to see a medical doctor. Some scholars believe that Paul and Luke had become acquainted earlier, because the leading medical school of that day was in Paul's hometown of Tarsus. Others suggest that Paul simply asked about a good doctor and was referred to Luke (who was a *brilliant* doctor). However it happened, I am convinced that Paul saw Luke to get treatment for his ailment.

While there, Paul (as usual) shared Christ and His Gospel with this brilliant Gentile doctor and "God turned on the lights" in his inner spirit. Dr. Luke became a Christian. He was radically convicted of his sins and converted to the Savior. Of course, Paul immediately began discipling him. But, the time was far too short.

Paul and Silas were "under orders." They were on a mission, and their itinerary and schedule were determined by the Holy Spirit. Paul gently said to Luke, "My brother, we must go now." Luke probably replied, "Go? *Go*? You just arrived, and you have led me to the greatest thing I have ever known or experienced, eternal life in Jesus Christ, and now you must go? This can't be!"

But when Paul insisted, Luke pondered the situation for some while and then he said, "Paul, how would you like to have another traveling companion on your missionary team?" Paul's spiritual enthusiasm mounted, but he realistically replied, "What a glorious possibility! But what about your medical practice?" Luke replied calmly, "Oh, that wouldn't be any great obstacle. The practice is in great shape. I could dispose of it easily." Now Paul realized how serious Luke seemed to be. "Do you mean that you would sell your practice and come along with us on the remainder of this journey? I can hardly believe it." "But Paul," said Luke, "you need a medical doctor regularly right now, and I need you at least as much as you need me. Yes, I'll do it!"

Do you think I am manufacturing these ideas? Well, I'm not. Up to verse 10 of Acts 16, the historian's (Luke's) narrative says, "They," as he writes *about* the missionary team; but at Acts 16:10 (concerning Troas, verse 8), the narrative says, "Immediately we endeavored to go into Macedonia"; and thus the "we sections" of Acts begin. Luke, the writer of the Book of Acts, joined Paul's team at Troas!

DEVOTIONAL TRUTHS

Let me interrupt our story to see some tremendous devotional truths. You see, disciple-making is never a one-way street. While Paul is discipling Titus, Titus is comforting Paul (II Corinthians 7:5-6). While Paul is imparting his veteran wisdom to young Timothy, young Timothy is supplying his youthful idealism to the aging Paul. While Paul is discipling Dr. Luke in Christ's life, Dr. Luke is imparting his medical knowledge and expertise to Paul the theologian.

Did you ever wonder where Paul humanly got his analogy of the Church as the very "Body of Christ"? From a human standpoint, is there really any question? Luke would naturally talk about the marvelous workings of the miraculous human body. He would explain the incredible human physical machine as he treated Paul's infirmity—as in other settings as well.

Perhaps he said one day, "Paul, how much intelligence do you have in your body below your chin? How much wisdom do you have in your body below the head?" Paul would reply, "I hadn't thought much about it previously, but the obvious answer is 'none.'" "That's correct," said Luke, "but then how do the members of your body below the chin know what to do if they have no wisdom or intelligence in themselves? The answer is another miracle in the body.

"You see, you have a system of nerves in your body which connect the members with the brain. The nerves which go out from the brain to the body members are called 'efferent nerves,' and the nerves which make the return trip are called 'afferent nerves.' The brain flashes orders down the efferent nerves to the members of the body, and if the body is healthy, the members obey instantly and flash an unconscious message up the afferent nerves back to the brain, 'Mission accomplished.' See my right hand extended here just now? The palm is up and the fingers spread. And it will maintain that posture until I release it to do otherwise. Why? Because the neurological connection between mind and member is healthy and functional."

All the time Luke is speaking, the Holy Spirit is mightily moving in the mind of Paul. Suddenly he says, "That is precisely the way the church operates, also. Just as your body is the vehicle of your self-expression, the church is Christ's body, and is the vehicle of His self-expression." And the Holy Spirit continues to expound the doctrine of the church as

Christ's body to Paul, the theologian, through Luke, the first medical missionary!

Some long time later, this Gentile medical doctor, Luke, discipled personally and extensively by the great Christian statesman, Paul, wrote two incredible documents which are found today in our New Testament. How did this happen? And what does it reveal to us about the disciple-making mandate of the Great Commission?

Get ready for this massive truth: Though Luke wrote only two documents of the twenty-seven in the New Testament, *those two documents make up roughly one-fourth of the volume of the New Testament.* What were they written for? Did Dr. Luke have an idea that these two documents would ever appear in a Bible? In the New Testament? Surely not, for he didn't even know a "New Testament" was to be published. Then why did he write these two incredible documents?

PERSONAL DISCIPLE IDENTIFIED

ONE-FOURTH OF THE NEW TESTAMENT WAS WRITTEN TO ONE PERSON!

Let's consider, secondly, the *personal disciple* to whom both these documents were written. The disciple's name is Theophilus. This name sounds peculiar to us. In fact, names are often peculiar to us. One little boy was asked his name by his first grade teacher. He replied, "6 and 7/8." Astonished, she asked, "Where did you ever get a name like that?" He answered, "My Daddy just drew it out of a hat." Another teacher asked a lively little boy his name, and he answered, "My name is Johnny, Don't." An Indian chief once went into the nearby township and said to the judge, "Me wantum change name." The judge asked, "What is your present name?" The chief replied, "Chief Screeching Train Whistle." "And what do you want to change it to?" "Toots."

A family had a new baby. After months of seeking a name for the baby and apparently choosing an attractive name, they gave him the strange name "Theophilus," after the baby was born. "Why?" a friend asked. "Why, after your earlier choice, did you finally give him the name 'Theophilus?" The father wryly replied, "We named him Theophilus because he was *the awfulest* looking baby we ever saw!"

This man's name, Theophilus, is a compound Greek word. The first part, "Theos," means "God. " The last part, "philos," means "love." So, his name either means "lover of God," or "beloved of God." Because of this meaning, some interpreters have said that this is likely not an individual person at all, but rather a category of people. But this simply is not so. The recipient is carefully described as a person in the first chapter of the Gospel of Luke.

Remember that the Gospel according to Luke and the Book of Acts both had the same *writer*, the same *recipient*, and essentially the same *subject.*

Now our second massive truth: *One-fourth of the New Testament was written to one person!* Here is the genius of the Gospel of Christ in boldfaced print! The Gospel of Christ maximizes the value, the purpose, the meaning, the usefulness, and the responsibility of each individual. If you want to see how far we have strayed from the ideal and impetus of the Biblical Gospel, ask yourself this question: Have you heard of anyone recently who has written a document of any length and sent it to just one person to reach that person for Christ?

On a clear, bright sunny day take a powerful magnifying glass and a stack of newspapers and go outside for an experiment. Crumple up several pages of the newspaper. Now, hold the magnifying glass over a pile of the crumpled pages. Even though you are magnifying the power of the sun's rays through the glass lens, you will never start a fire—if you keep moving the glass. But if you hold the magnifying glass still, on just one point, allowing it to focus the rays into a concentrated beam of the sun's energy, you will harness the power of the sun and start a fire. And the fire always spreads to everything around it that is combustible! In our story, Jesus is the sun, Luke is the magnifying glass, and Theophilus is the one personal point on which everything is focused. And the fire is burning and spreading still!

WHY DID LUKE WRITE THESE TWO DOCUMENTS TO ONE PERSON?

Back to our earlier question: Why did Luke write these two documents to this one person? Do we have any way of knowing? Yes, we do.

What was the condition of Theophilus when Luke wrote his Gospel to him? He was quite apparently a lost man, an unsaved sinner. Luke addresses him as "most excellent Theophilus" (Luke 1:3). This is a Greek nobleman's title, so Theophilus was a Greek nobleman, a man of rank and position. *No Christian is ever addressed by such a title in the New Testament*, so this man was a lost man. He had apparently heard the Gospel (Luke 1:4), but was unconvinced. Remember that "the Greeks seek after wisdom" (I Corinthians 1:22), and are not easily convinced of ideas which may sound so humanly unreasonable as the Gospel (on first consideration). So, Theophilus balked at the truth when it was presented to him. But Luke was also a Gentile, and Luke had also had intellectual problems with the Gospel. But Luke had become perfectly convinced of the authenticity and integrity of Jesus Christ and His Gospel, so he undertook to write an orderly presentation of the facts of Jesus and the Gospel to this unconvinced man, Theophilus.

What was Luke's purpose of writing? *To win this one man to faith in Christ!* Lengthy research, laborious work, and tedious writing—*all for one man*—that he might "know the certainty of those things, wherein he had been instructed." Did the Gospel of Luke accomplish this purpose? Yes, it did! How do we know? Because in the very first line of the second document, Luke drops the title of rank and simply calls him "Theophilus." So, the great task of evangelism was accomplished in this case in this peculiar way. One Greek medical doctor, a brilliant professional man, researched the Gospel perfectly and wrote an apologetic Gospel to a serious Greek nobleman to convince him about Jesus and to bring him to Christ and salvation. And it happened.

Then why did Luke write this second document, the Book of Acts (another 28 chapters in your New Testament)? If the man was won to Christ by the first document, then why is a second one necessary? Friends, the answer to this question discloses the tragic sinful default of the modern church. The purpose of Christ has but barely begun when a person is saved! It is His intention to implicate each of His followers, all born-again believers, in *world-visionary, world-impacting disciple-making.* It is His design that each believer be a *reproducer of reproducers* with the "uttermost parts of the earth" continually in mind. It is His intention that we follow His pattern—*to see the masses through the man, and build the man to impact the masses.* So, the Book of the Acts was written by Dr.

Luke to introduce Theophilus, in concept and conduct, to the world-moving strategy of Jesus.

Did it work? Did Theophilus become a visionary disciple-maker, a reproducer of reproducers? We simply don't know, and that is all the better, because it means that every believer must be given maximum chance *through personal enlistment, personal equipment, and personal deployment*—whether he "produces" or not. We do have some evidence that Theophilus was captured by the mandate to make disciples—after all, we are reading the Book of Acts today! So, Luke wrote a second lengthy document (28 chapters in your Bible) to indoctrinate the mind and infect the heart and invite the participation of *one man* in the greatest work in the world.

If the Holy Spirit of God models this qualitative involvement in the lives of individuals in the New Testament, should I not continually have at least a small group of individuals into whom I am pouring my life and my vision? Should I not live with a burning Great Commission consciousness and seek to share it qualitatively with groups of "faithful men who will be able to teach others, also" (II Timothy 2:2)?

PERSONAL TESTIMONY

I will risk a personal testimony at this point. With a vision that has been erratically enlarging for over a quarter of a century, I have spent large amounts of time with many individuals, with many small groups, with many groups of pastors and missionaries, and with many entire churches, seeking to impart this standard. I have seen magnificent successes so that people whom I have influenced are now in far-flung parts of the world—winning and training disciples; and I have sadly seen numerous failures (and have failed myself in ways which surely have grieved the Holy Spirit). I could fill many pages with easily verifiable accounts of disciples who have gone out to reproduce this standard in their fields of service. Quite a number of them are pastors (and I have had the great privilege of teaching and encouraging many more pastors who are established in the ministry), some are missionaries to foreign countries, and many are "lay people" with a living vision to make disciples where they live, work, and worship. I am grateful to God for this matchless privilege, and am more committed today than ever before to "turn men into disciples."

PLAIN DECLARATION OF PURPOSE FOR WRITING

ALL THAT JESUS BEGAN BOTH TO DO AND TO TEACH

Now we consider the final division of our outline of Acts 1:1, the *plain declaration of purpose* for writing the first document, the Gospel of Luke. Luke says that it concerned "all that Jesus began both to do and to teach." Note the three verbs, "began," "do," and "teach." The last two verbs form a descriptive overlook of Jesus' entire ministry. Jesus is the only person in history who had perfect balance between the Divinely-desired doing and teaching. In every other ministry, whether that of a church or that of an individual Christian, there has been some measure of imbalance between the two.

Think of the churches you are acquainted with. Some are heavily over-balanced in favor of *doing*. Their modus operandi seems to be "get saved and get busy." They are heavy on *activity* but light on *academics*. They are forward on *performance* but backward on *principle and precept*. One man expressed to me a caricature of his own church by saying, "Brother Herb, you'll find that our church is about 5 miles wide and about a quarter of an inch deep." He meant that rushing activity is constantly enlarging the numbers in the church, but that spiritual depth has not kept pace with the numerical growth.

On the other hand, there are churches that are heavily overbalanced in favor of *teaching*. They are constantly being fed on the Word of God, but there is no suitable balance in aggressive active ministries. The members of these churches tend to develop "hardening of the hearteries," a kind of sluggish smugness that may tilt over into articulate self-righteousness. These churches have some salving growth, but the Great Commission is certainly not the overwhelming agenda in them. They will argue the identification of the third toe of the left foot of Daniel's image, but give no real attention to the billions of people who remain unevangelized in our world.

Jesus had perfect balance between doing and teaching in His ministry, and each of us should prayerfully seek for this balance in our lives and in the churches which we attend and in which we serve.

This brings us to the "big" verb in Acts 1:1, the word "began." The Gospel of Luke concerned "all that Jesus began both *to do and to teach*." Those historical events in the life of Jesus which are mentioned earlier are only a beginning! Presumably then, if the "former treatise" concerned what Jesus "*began* to do and teach," then the present document, the Book of Acts, will be about all that Jesus is *continuing* to do and teach. But this creates an immediate problem. Midway in the first chapter of the Acts, the "doer and teacher," Jesus, disappears from sight! Then how did He *continue* to do and teach through twenty-seven and one half more chapters if He is gone from their sight?

WHAT IS JESUS DOING NOW?

Let's enlarge the question. What is Jesus doing now? He is continuing to do and teach to the level of His intent and purpose in our world today just as He did when He was here in the days of His flesh. But how is He doing it if He is not visible? He is doing it in the same manner He followed when He was here in His own physical body. What was His method then? We call it "incarnation," which means that "the Word (the 'logos,' the logic of God) became flesh and dwelt among us." So, God came down to our level in the human Person of His Son, Jesus, and lived, performed and taught among men. What is His method today? Exactly the same, with these modifications:

1. He occupies the bodies of all born-again believers for the purpose of extending His doing and teaching through them;

2. Unlike Jesus, each of them (us) is a sinner;

3. There is a qualitative difference in that none of us is Jesus. He is uniquely the only-one-of-a-kind Son of God.

With these modifications, each believer is to be an extension of the incarnation of Jesus Christ! The instant a sinner is saved, Jesus Christ enters that person's inner life by the Presence and power of the Holy Spirit. The Holy Spirit has been described as "Jesus' Other Self," and may be loosely understood as "Jesus without a body." So, each believer is a living container of the Personal Presence of the Son of God, and a primary purpose for this is that the believer may be an ongoing extension of the doings and teachings of Jesus.

WHAT KIND OF PERSONS DID JESUS USE?

This raises another question, a very vital one. What kind of persons did Jesus use in the Book of Acts to continue His doings and teachings after His Ascension? Interestingly enough, the opening verses of the Book of Acts provide a perfect answer to this question. These verses provide an excellent profile of Christ's earliest followers. Let's reconstruct a portrait of His first followers.

1. COMMON MEN

First, they were *common men.* We have only to be reminded of all we know of them from the Gospels to know this. They were a cross-section of society, the most common of men. All except one were from Galilee, and that one exception was "the rotten egg in the dozen," Judas Iscariot. Galilee was a despised tiny province of the Roman Empire, and eleven of Jesus' first men originated there. They were "a bunch of zeroes," and out of them He made His heroes. This should make each of us very comfortable, because Jesus Christ does not require anything of us for the accomplishment of His purpose through us except the yieldedness of our common clay.

2. CHOSEN MEN

Then, these were *chosen men.* Look at verse 2 in Acts 1. His first men are called "the Apostles whom He had chosen." What were they chosen for? The word "*apostles*" gives us a great insight. The word "apostle" means "one sent on a mission." He chose them so that He could send them wherever He wanted them to go in order that they might be, say, and do anything He wanted! And this is why He chose you and me! Note the word, "chosen," at the end of verse two. Every Greek verb "travels" in one of three voices: the active voice, the passive voice, and the middle voice. In the active voice, *the subject acts through the verb*, such as "I run," "I stand," "you walk," "you talk." In each case, the subject acts through the verb. The passive voice means *the subject is acted upon through the verb*, such as "I was run over!" The middle voice combines the other two voices so that the *subject acts through the verb*, but in such a way that *the result of the action comes back to the subject himself*. The action is like that of a boomerang when it is thrown. I heard of a man who bought himself a new boomerang—but he killed himself trying to throw the old one away!

This verb, "chosen," is a middle voice verb and presents to us a stupendous truth. It means that when God chose you, He chose you, not merely for your own advantage—your health, wealth, and happiness, but for *His own sake*! You are saved *for God's sake*! You are a Christian *for Christ's sake*! You are alive for His sake! So you are not a Christian to get your needs met, or to *gratify* and satisfy yourself, but to be employed and deployed by Jesus Christ as a continuation point of His ongoing doing and teaching.

When I was a boy, my father taught me a great love for the game of baseball. My awareness of the game came from my father, and my competitiveness came from my mother. The neighborhood boys often played baseball on Saturdays in the vacant lot next to our house. I can remember my anger at the team captains when week after week I didn't get chosen and, thus, didn't get to play. But, I also remember the first day I got to play. There were not enough players and someone had to choose me! It didn't take me long to figure out that the captain who chose me didn't choose me just because he liked me. ***He chose me primarily because he felt that his choice of me would help his side win the game.***

Do you see the application of the illustration? Jesus Christ does love me, and there is nothing I can do to cause Him to stop! He doesn't love me because I am loveable, lovely, or loving. He loves me because He is love—period. But, He did not choose me merely because He loved me, as massive as His love is. He chose me (also) because He felt that His choice of me would help His side win the game! Is my participation in His global mission such that it would "justify" His choice of me? Or am I "at ease in Zion," a total misrepresentation of Christ's global purpose?

Every Christian reading these words should pause right now and say to himself, "I have been picked out by the King of all Kings! I have been hand-selected by the Lord of glory! Am I fulfilling the purpose for which He selected me?"

3. CONVINCED MEN

Then, they were *convinced men.* Acts 1:3 says that "Jesus showed Himself alive to them after His death by many infallible proofs (unanswerable evidences), being seen by them forty days." The word "seen" translates the Greek word from which we get our medical terms "ophthalmia," "ophthalmology," and "ophthalmologist." It is the technical root word for the human eyeball. So, it could be accurately translated, "Jesus was *eyeballed* by them forty days"—after His death and resurrection! Later, one of them wrote, "We have seen with our eyes the Word of Life" (I John 1:1).

Also, there is another feature of this brief phrase from Acts 1:3 that needs careful attention. There is a tiny preposition in the text that is very difficult to translate in English. It is the Greek word "dia," and is translated "between." Jesus was "seen by them *between* forty days." What a peculiar expression! What does it mean? It means that His visibility to the apostles was not continuous for the entire forty days. He appeared and disappeared at His own will for those forty days. He materialized to sight and de-materialized to invisibility as He desired during those forty days.

Suppose that I and a friend were engaged, even engrossed, in conversation. Our eyes are fixed on one another. But, *suddenly* another human body materializes between us! Friends, that would scare whatever is in you right out! No wonder Jesus typically began His communication with "Fear not," or "Peace be unto you." Now, both my friend and I become totally oblivious to our previous conversation and completely occupied with the "intruding" person. And suppose, while we are transfixed by him, he just as suddenly disappears, de-materializing out of our sight? This is what happened over and over in the forty-day period after His resurrection. Jesus hop-scotched back and forth from visibility to invisibility again and again during those forty days.

What a peculiar thing! Why did He do that? *He wanted His disciples to know without doubt or question that He was no less present with them when they couldn't see Him than He was when they could!* And the same is true today. Jesus Christ is so much present in the Person of the Holy Spirit that He could materialize into bodily form—if He wished to. But His stated purpose is that *each believer* give Him "bodily form" by letting his own body be the "temple," the "Holy of Holies," the shrine through which Jesus exhibits Himself.

Don't you think you would be completely convinced if you saw Jesus the way they did? Be very careful. Jesus Himself indicated that, because of the indwelling Presence of the Holy Spirit, the advantage belongs to us and not to the earliest believers (John 16:7).

How convinced are *you* about the reality of Jesus? About the validity of His claims? About the integrity of His Person? About His ability and His authority? About His universal missionary purpose? No great movement of God has ever occurred through unconvinced men. May God open our eyes freshly and fully to the Person and purpose of Jesus.

4. COMMANDED MEN

Then, they were *commanded men*. Acts 1:2 says that "Jesus through the Holy Spirit gave commandments" unto them. Verse 4 adds, "Being assembled together with them, Jesus commanded them that they should not depart from Jerusalem, but wait for the promise of the Father, which, saith He, ye have heard of me." The "promise of the Father" is a reference to the Day of Pentecost, the day of the full release of the Holy Spirit's redemptive power, a day which was then to follow very shortly.

Can you imagine what impulsive, self-aggressive Simon Peter might have thought at this point? "Jesus, why don't you make up your mind? You have spent three years preparing us to go, and now You tell us to wait!" But no such protest arose. By this time, the Apostles had learned not to argue with Jesus. After all, One Who is Absolute Lord of the universe is always right! Today's church should be so wise! It should spend a great deal of its time in prayer and Bible investigation to be convinced that it is operating exclusively by the Mind of Christ, then it should spend the rest of its time obeying Him.

The ancient Arabs created a special breed of horses, sometimes called "Arabian steeds." At first, they were bred for exclusive use in the King's stables. As part of the equestrian training, a trainer carried a whistle on a rawhide rope around his neck. For months the horse was trained to stop all activity at the sound of the trainer's whistle and make a "bee line" for the trainer. Rigid obedience was required. The tiniest refusal was total disobedience. Then, for five days food was withheld from the horse, and for three days the horse was refused water to drink. It was kept in a corral in these final days of training.

On the last day, a trough of food and water was placed visibly about one hundred yards from the corral. The horse would stampede in hunger and thirst on the trough side of the corral. Then suddenly, the corral door would be sprung open, and the surprised horse would gallop toward the trough. But, when the horse was yet about twenty-five yards from the trough, the trainer standing off to the side would blow the whistle! Everything about the horse would tighten in confusion. A choice had to quickly be made. The choice? Trough or trainer? Which would it be? If the horse continued to the trough and gratified its hunger and thirst, thus disobeying the command of the trainer, it would either be recycled through the process or dismissed altogether. If the horse voted against its own drives and instincts and in favor of the trainer and the training process, thus going immediately to the trainer, it was then dismissed to go to the trough for food and water.

Friends, every day such a choice confronts us. Trough of self gratification, or the Trainer's commands? These were commanded men, and Jesus expects nothing less from us.

5. CONTROLLED MEN

Finally, these were *controlled men.* In verse 4, Jesus spoke to them of "the promise of the Father," a promise concerning the coming of the Holy Spirit to empower His church on the Day of Pentecost.

In verse 5, He said, "Ye shall be baptized with the Holy Spirit not many days hence." The King James Bible used the old word "Ghost" instead of "Spirit," and in one great sense, I like that translation. A ghost (in our thinking) is the part of the person that remains behind when the body has departed. The Holy Spirit may be described as Jesus present without a body! So, the Holy Spirit will do the same things, pursue the same purposes, and build the same kind of people Jesus built when He was here in the flesh. If Jesus produced wild and fanatical men, so will the Holy Spirit. But Jesus didn't produce that kind of people. He produced men who were vocationally prepared, skilled, and involved. They were men who could re-present Him in any situation. They were men who skillfully handled the intricacies of the Word of God and applied it to every situation.

And now, since the Day of Pentecost, the Holy Spirit is our great "Stay-Within Friend," always present and willing to control and empower us for the Master's Mission. Are you filled with the great and gentle Holy Spirit, inwardly controlled by Him so that He can determine your character, speech, conduct, schedule, and itinerary?

Chapter 5
Essentials for Making Disciples
or
The Doctor's Cure for the Great Omission

"Forasmuch as many have taken in hand to set forth in order a declaration of those things which are most surely believed among us, Even as they delivered them unto us, which from the beginning were eyewitnesses, and ministers of the word; It seemed good to me also, having had perfect understanding of all things from the very first, to write unto thee in order, most excellent Theophilus, That thou mightest know the certainty of those things, wherein thou hast been instructed."

Luke 1: 1-4, King James Version

"Since (as is well known) many have undertaken to put in order and draw up a (thorough) narrative of the surely established deeds which have been accomplished and fulfilled in and among us, Exactly as they were handed down to us by those who from the (official) beginning (of Jesus' ministry) were eyewitnesses and ministers of the Word (that is, of the doctrine concerning the attainment through Christ of salvation in the kingdom of God). It seeming good and desirable to me, (I have

determined) also after having searched out diligently and followed all things closely and traced accurately the course from the highest to the minutest detail from the very first, to write an orderly account for you, most excellent Theophilus, (My purpose is) that you may know the full truth, and understand with certainty and security against error the accounts (histories) and doctrines of the faith of which you have been informed and in which you have been orally instructed."

Amplified Bible

"Since many writers have undertaken to compose narratives about the facts established among us, just as the original eye-witnesses who became ministers of the message have handed them down to us, I too, most excellent Theophilus, because I have carefully investigated them all from the start, have felt impressed to write them out in order for you, that you may better know the certainty of those things that you have been taught."

Williams translation

"The author to Theophilus: Many writers have undertaken to draw up an account of the events that have happened among us, following the traditions handed down to us by the original eyewitnesses and servants of the Gospel. And so I in my turn, your Excellency, as one who has gone over the whole course of these events in detail, have decided to write a connected narrative for you, so as to give you authentic knowledge about the matters of which you have been informed."

New English Bible

Psalm 119:18 records this prayer: "Open Thou mine eyes, that I might behold wondrous things out of Thy law." Let me urge you to pray this prayer continually for yourself as you read and study this chapter. Psalm 119:130 says, "The entrance of Thy Word gives light; it gives understanding to the simple." May this be so as we study together.

Let's begin our study by looking meditatively at the progression of this line:

WORD ► FLESH ► WORD ► FLESH ► WORD ► (put your name here) ► WORD ► FLESH.

This progression represents the manner of Gospel advance among men throughout the history of the Christian movement (Romans 10:14). It began with the "Word," the "Logos," becoming flesh and dwelling among men (John 1:14). Every advance thereafter is a modified form of the same formula, the Word becoming flesh. In process of time, by a miracle of God's grace and power, His salvation was "in-fleshed" in you. At that point, your name went into the progression as suggested in the line above—and both your destiny and your vocation changed forever. Now a practical question arises. Since your name has been entered into the progression, will the progression from the past to the future continue through you? Or will the link break with you at the time of your death? Will it look like this: FLESH ►WORD ►FLESH .... ? Will the intended progression end with you?

Face the question again: Will the progression continue through history because of the role you played in your slot while you were alive? If the progression is to continue with you, there is a vocation which you must learn, and it is already prescribed for you in the Word of God. If you only win another person to Christ, the link will probably break with the person you win. If you win someone and train him without a full awareness and implementation of "the standard" (of world-visionary, world-impacting multiplicative disciple-making), the progression will probably break with the person you win and train. Indeed, you will only make him a "better Christian." It is only when you win and train someone according to the revealed Biblical standard that God will guarantee that the chain will not break, and you yourself will guarantee its continuation by laying the foundation for many generations.

The Gospel of Luke, written by the only Gentile writer of Scripture, is a monumental text which breathes through and through with world-impacting disciple-making. World-visionary, world-impacting disciple-making is the standard of Gospel advance in the New Testament. Keep in mind that Luke was not an apostle, not a preacher, not an evangelist, not even an ordained deacon. Luke was a Gentile, a scientist, a medical doctor and an amateur historian made infallible by the inspiration of the Holy Spirit. Pause over the word "amateur" in the preceding sentence. The word certainly fits Luke as an historian. The word describes a person who engages in an activity for the sheer *love* of it. Dr. Luke stands forever as one of the greatest examples of the **WORD TO FLESH TO WORD** standard of the New Testament. The first four verses of the Gospel according to Luke form an introduction to the document, and seem (by the grammatical wording of the text) to have been written after the body of the document was completed. In these verses, we may see one of greatest examples of disciple-making in the Bible.

In his remarkable introduction, Dr. Luke demonstrates four essential characteristics of a world-visionary, world-impacting, multiplying disciple-maker. Any disciple who is to experience the reality of God's big vision for himself, his generation, and future generations, must incarnate these four characteristics in his own life and must, in turn, build them into any disciple God gives to him.

Dr. Luke accepted *personal responsibility* for building Theophilus, engaged in *painstaking research* on behalf of Theophilus, developed *precise resources* to equip Theophilus, and did everything humanly possible to generate *persistent reproduction* of other world-visionary, world-impacting, multiplying disciples through Theophilus. Read this last sentence with great care, giving it much thought. "Consider what I say, and the Lord give thee understanding in all things" (II Timothy 2:7).

PERSONAL RESPONSIBILITY

If you are to follow the New Testament standard, *you must take personal responsibility for building people into New Testament disciples.*

Luke began by acknowledging the commendable efforts of others to compose an account of Jesus' life and ministry. Though others had put forth extreme effort and hard work to draw up a narrative of Jesus, Luke said, "It seemed good to *me* also..." The Holy Spirit was working through Luke to do much more than Luke could imagine. *Luke* saw *one* man—Theophilus. *God saw many generations, including us!* Luke wrote one document to one man. *God prepared an incredible Gospel for all future generations!* We may only see a disciple, but God sees the masses the disciple will impact.

The history of the Christian church proves that this Divine concept is tragically easy for human minds to miss. *If you do not make disciples, you disagree with the standard of Jesus and disobey the command of Jesus. If you do not build your disciples to the point of world-visionary, world impacting, consummate, reproducing disciple-making, you have not agreed with nor conformed to the standard of Jesus—regardless of whatever else may be true of your life!* The Gospel itself is predicated upon agreement with God (Romans 10:9; Matthew 10:32, where "confession" means agreement with) concerning our complete *lack of conformity* to His standard. Then, we are brought by the Holy Spirit to agree with God's assessment of His Son, Jesus. Our entire life thereafter is to be an agreement with God and His will. When we examine His command and His standard for making disciples, we see that it isn't enough for an individual Christian to just start ministering to people, being nice to people, seeking to meet people's needs, or just be a good, faithful churchgoer. We must choose against ourselves ("deny ourselves," Matthew 16:24) and fully agree with God. And since we are told to fulfill the Commission of Jesus "as we are going," we must not take one more step without implementing both His Mandate and His Method for fulfilling it.

Consider the words of our Master in John 15:16: "You (major emphasis) did not choose Me, but I (major emphasis) chose you, and appointed you, that you (major emphasis) should go and bear (continuous action) fruit (major emphasis) and that your fruit should remain (present infinitive), that whatever you ask of the Father in My name, He may give to you." What is the practical use of fruit? A tree which bears fruit never eats its own fruit; it is for *someone else.* One part of the fruit is for food, but the other part is for reproduction. The seed in the fruit perpetuates the process of the production of food and the reproduction of fruit. How many seeds are there in a mango? Only one! How many mangos are in one mango seed? Only God knows!

You have been brought into the Kingdom of God *to take personal responsibility for the next available man.* Yet, there is nothing automatic about it! Today you will cross paths with countless people in the crowds of life who might be available to the disciple-making process (given the right enlistment, information and training)—and you might not even notice a single one of them. Unless you "see and hear" *from God 's point of view* you will never fulfill your personal responsibility for the next available man.

May I remind you that the question, "Am I my brother's keeper?" was addressed to God from the self-defensive and hate-filled heart of the world's first murderer! If I do not join Jesus in assuming personal responsibility for building the next available man for world impact, I necessarily side with the sentiment of a murderer. The Divine answer to Cain's question is, "Yes, you are your brother's keeper. More importantly, you are your brother's *brother*!" So how are you doing with your Abel? May you say with Luke, "It seemed good to me, also. I assume personal responsibility for the man God has given me."

PAINSTAKING RESEARCH

If you are to follow the New Testament standard, *you must engage in painstaking research of the Word for the sake of your disciple.* Jesus said, "For their sakes, I sanctify Myself," and your life must echo His. It is not enough to simply study the Bible. There are people everywhere involved in Bible studies who will never build one reproducing disciple-maker who will impact the world. Why? The reason is simple: neither the perception of the teacher of the Bible nor the student of the Bible accommodates a vision for world impact. Those involved in the Bible study do not see it as a means for world impact nor do they form curriculum from the Bible study to intentionally build world impacters. Instead, they study the Bible to merely "learn more" and to be "better Christians." It is even questionable as to whether those are worthy motives for a Christian. They smack too much of the "consumer friendly" Christianity, or the "tupperware mentality," of the western church. Most tragic of all, this produces *terminal intake* of the Gospel, instead of *germinal planting* which will reproduce vast spiritual harvests to the ends of the earth until the end of time. Anyone can read the Bible for himself. However, world impact only emerges from the lives of those who intentionally engage in diligent research for the purpose of truly knowing and following Christ and making Him known to others.

Look at Luke 1:3 and notice the word "investigated" (NIV/NAS). This word carries the same intensity as "rightly dividing" in II Timothy 2:15 and is the same word as "fully known" in II Timothy 3:10, where Paul said to Timothy, "You have fully known my doctrine, manner of life, purpose, faith, longsuffering, charity, patience...." The Greek word in Luke 1:3 and in II Timothy 3:10 is *parakolutheo*, which means "to accompany side by side, to follow closely, to attend to carefully." Metaphorically, *parakolutheo* means *to follow closely a mental trail clearly set forth by one who has frequently traveled the terrain, investigating every detail and leaving no stone unturned.* Let the reader meditate at length on this last sentence. Again, "consider what I say, and the Lord give you understanding in all things" (II Timothy 2:7). The mental trail or course in the text is comprised of the actual events involving Jesus Christ from eternity to eternity. When Jesus left Heaven and entered time and space, He blazed a trail in the hard and fast terrain of history. Each Christian is to mentally and spiritually follow that trail, investigating every detail so that he can reproduce the details in his own life and build from these details both a course and a curriculum for his own disciples. This will require painstaking research.

The word *parakolutheo* carries another shade of meaning. It means "to trace." The idea is conveyed in the tracing of an outline or a picture by a child. The child overlays the picture he wants to reproduce with a thin sheet of paper and methodically and meticulously traces every line, every stroke, every shade. The finished product is then a carbon copy bearing the image of the original—down to the minutest detail. So Luke sets out to trace the character and reproduce the heart and passion of Jesus of Nazareth. When Luke removed the writing instrument from the last page of his Gospel, the beauty of Jesus, His humanity and His compassion for mankind stood revealed in radiant splendor. Luke's finished product is unlike that of any other Gospel writer. It was the Holy Spirit Who guided each movement of Luke's pen to trace out the image of God in the humanity of Jesus. We, too, are to follow Luke's guidance in tracing out the character of Jesus, the course He followed, and the curriculum He used in impacting men—and we are to go and do likewise!

Earlier, we mentioned II Timothy 2:15. The Greek word used there and translated, "rightly dividing" in the King James Version, is closely related to *parakolutheo.* It is the word *orthotomeo.* Ponder this word for a moment. Think of the other words you know that begin with the prefix, *ortho.* Orthodontics means, "straight teeth," or "right teeth." Orthopedics means "straight bones," or "right bones." The term *orthotomeo* is a compound Greek word, *orthos* meaning "right," and "temno" meaning "to cut, to divide, to handle skillfully." Luke was surely a very competent and skilled medical doctor, one who had been made acutely aware of the crucial importance of technical details through his vocation. Luke understood that if one sign or symptom went undetected, it could mean death to his patient. He was a responsible steward of skills and information and applications in dealing with life-and-death matters. And he knew that his present subject was a life-and-death, heaven-and-hell matter!

The best historical research indicates that Luke was scientifically trained at the medical school at Tarsus (in fact, some scholars have suggested that Paul, Luke, and Theophilus may all have been *fellow-students* at the university there), and thus he had received the best available training in the medical field at that time. At any rate, it is quite possible that Luke, a stellar medical student, knew Saul, an accomplished scribe and theologian, before they met in the Book of Acts (Acts 16). It would seem that Paul, due to a serious medical problem (the Book of Galatians suggests a very serious eye problem), went to obtain the services of Dr. Luke. It seems probable that Paul (perhaps in the course of the visit) shared Christ and the Gospel with Dr. Luke. While Luke was treating Paul's eyes to correct their deficient vision, God the Holy Spirit broke into the darkness of Luke's *spiritual blindness* with "the light of the glorious Gospel of Christ, who is the image of God" (II Corinthians 4:4). The same "God, who commanded the light to shine out of darkness" shone into the doctor's heart, "to give the light of the knowledge of the glory of God in the face of Jesus Christ" (II Corinthians 4:6)! A short while later, when Paul announced his intentions to depart from Troas with his missionary team to another assigned destination, Luke asked to accompany him. Paul might have said, "But Doctor, you have your medical practice here; you can't just leave it!" And Dr. Luke might have answered, "No, but it is a good practice, and I can easily put it in someone else's hands." So Luke disposed of his medical practice and joined the Apostle Paul on his remaining missionary journeys!

Luke was the only Gospel writer who was professionally trained in the art of medical science. Now Luke turns all of his scientific training and expertise to advantage in gathering the facts of the story of Christ from those who were eye-witnesses of Jesus. Through his travels with Paul, and surely through some independent traveling of his own, he met these eye-witnesses in Asia Minor, in various parts of Palestine, and especially at Jerusalem. Little by little, Luke's notebooks began to bulge from the many personal interviews he conducted. Incidentally, it is almost a rule of thumb: One true mark of a visionary disciple-maker is an ever-enlarging, bulging notebook! Luke's notebook was filled with what Jesus said and what He did. Whenever Luke met anyone who had spent time with Jesus, had met Jesus or observed His miracles, He would ask key investigative questions: "Did you personally know Jesus?" "What was Jesus doing when you saw Him?" "What did Jesus say?" "Tell me everything that you know about Him." Some of the people he questioned closely were Peter, James, John and others of the original twelve Apostles. He most certainly conferred with John Mark, who may have been completing his Gospel (the Gospel of Mark) at the time. There is much strong evidence that Luke had substantial conversation with Mary, the mother of Jesus. The Doctor wrote most extensively of all Biblical writers on the virgin birth of Christ, and medical doctors aren't easily convinced of virgin births! A writer named William Hobart wrote an extensive book concerning the medical language of Dr. Luke, in which he points out over four hundred distinctive technical medical terms which Luke used in composing his Gospel and the Book of Acts. The Doctor became perfectly convinced of the virgin birth of Christ on the basis of powerful and unanswerable evidence. He received great insight into Jesus' birth through interviews with Mary herself.

Now, with scientific precision, the skilled physician set forth an orderly account of the Master's life. He gives an extensive and detailed report of His birth, His life and teachings, His death, His resurrection, some events of the forty days after His resurrection, and His ascension. Luke clearly made great effort to research the Person, teaching, deeds and accomplishments of Jesus. In Luke 1:3, the word "perfect" is the Greek word *akribos*, which means "diligent," "careful," or "circumspect." Luke researched Jesus from the top (*akron*, the topmost point; compare the word "Acropolis," which means, "high city") to the bottom (*abussas* or "abyss"). "Theophilus," Luke says, "I have spared no effort in researching Jesus from the highest detail to the deepest truth." Luke was confident that he had given his best effort to research every detail of Jesus' life—from top to bottom.

The four Gospels of the New Testament were not written in a sterile vacuum, but in the rough and tumble of life. Though each Gospel is inspired of the Holy Spirit, it nonetheless has upon it the distinctive earmarks and eccentricities of its human writer. John still sounds like John, Mark sounds like Mark, Matthew sounds like Matthew—even if each is writing a document that is perfect, and even if each document concerns a perfect Subject. In Luke 1:1, the Doctor said that his account contained things concerning Jesus that were totally and completely accomplished right before the eyes of those he interviewed. Another Gospel writer, the Apostle John, said in his first general letter that these eyewitnesses had *seen*, *heard*, and *touched* Jesus. Thus, they presented the evidence of *visible, audible and tangible testimony*. The Greek word for "eyewitnesses"in Luke 1:1 is *autoptes*, a compound word which means "self-see." It's the same root word from which we get the word "autopsy," which means that the examiner sees for himself the real cause of a person's death. The accounts that Luke heard from these eyewitnesses were so powerfully persuasive to him that he was confident they would persuade, convince, and satisfy anyone who would investigate them fully. In the Book of Acts, he refers to them as "many infallible proofs," or "unanswerable evidences" (Acts 1:3). He writes his Gospel to present the compelling evidence of these accounts.

Furthermore, Luke tells us that he had solicited information and testimony from the original ministers of Christ, many of whom had given their lives or would give their lives soon thereafter, sealing their testimony concerning Jesus with their life's blood. The word "ministers" in Luke 1:2 is the Greek word *huperetes*, which means "an under-rower." This word was used for a galley slave on board a ship, one who occupied the lowest place *to deliver someone else to his desired destination.*

A galley slave was carried to the bottom of the ship and chained there with only one vocation. His only assignment was to behold the cadence captain and row in unison by the captain's command with the other slaves. These "ministers" were so convinced concerning the Person and majesty of Jesus Christ that they became galley slaves on the "good ship of Grace," living to behold and obey the Captain, the Lord Jesus Christ. Their only purpose was *to deliver someone else to his final destination.* Luke powerfully demonstrates this vocation and lifestyle when he researched the story of Jesus and wrote this *incredible* (***incredible!***) document to deliver one man, Theophilus, to a desirable destiny in this life and a desirable destination in the life to come. Both the Gospel of Luke and the Book of Acts bleed through and through with the disciple-maker's paradigm—**somebody else, somebody else, somebody else**... Every Christian should see himself as a locked-in galley slave, doing whatever is necessary to master this Gospel, follow its directions, develop a curriculum, and build disciples, all in order to get *somebody else* to his final destination.

PRECISE RESOURCES

If you are to follow the New Testament standard, *you must develop precise resources to build other disciples.* Luke had promised to give Theophilus an orderly, detailed written account of the Gospel of Jesus Christ. Here in verse one Luke uses a military term, *anatassomai,* which means a placing of soldiers, or things, or facts, into their proper order. Luke sought to place the truths concerning Jesus in proper order like an army of soldiers arrayed and arranged for total world conquest. Luke reminded Theophilus that he had researched Jesus from top to bottom and placed his findings in "consecutive order." No thinking disciple can escape Luke's clear purpose to precisely systematize a curriculum for maximum efficiency in the life of another.

Luke, like Paul his discipler, set out to build men who could rightly divide the Scriptures—*orthoscripturists,* you might call them (II Timothy 2:15). Paul told Timothy in II Timothy 3:10 that "you have fully known my doctrine." Paul had systematically arranged the great truths of the Gospel so Timothy could fully grasp them and be anchored firmly to them, and correctly reproduce them in somebody else. Luke was discipled by Paul and now Luke provides a perfect example of the rule of Jesus, who said, "When the process is completed, the disciple will be like his teacher" (Luke 6:40). Also, Luke profiles in these verses the perfect example of a disciple building a curriculum to make other disciples. He had "compiled an accurate account" and "in consecutive order" of the facts about Jesus for the sake of indoctrinating, enlisting, building, and deploying one man to world impact. F. F. Bruce states that "this expression points to a connected series of narratives in order, topical or chronological, rather than mere isolated narratives." Prior to this letter, Luke (or *some other Christian*) had "instructed" (Luke 1:4) Theophilus by verbal witness concerning Jesus. The word *katecheo* is the Greek word from which we derive the word "catechize," or the word "catechism," which means to *instruct systematically*, especially by questions, answers, explanations and corrections. Luke demonstrates the absolute necessity for both a systematic verbal presentation of the Gospel to win the disciple to Christ, and a systematic written curriculum for building the disciple in the faith and the Christian vocation.

Luke did all this in order that Theophilus would come to a full, complete understanding of Jesus Christ resulting in an unshakable certainty concerning Him. Alfred Plummer commented on the word "certainty" in verse four, "Theophilus will know that the Gospel has an impregnable historical foundation." We, too, should begin formulating a curriculum and forming an illustration file (compare the parables of Jesus which Luke records in his Gospel), using every Scripturally sound item we can find to build our disciples upon the unshakable foundation of the glorious Gospel of our Lord Jesus Christ.

There are many good, well-meaning, knowledgeable Christians who will not intentionally build one world-visionary, world-impacting, reproducing disciple. Why? They will never take seriously their responsibility to build (or find) a systematic, precise curriculum for the purpose of getting *someone else* to his final destination. Lest a "layman" should seek to dodge this truth, F. F. Bruce reminds us that Luke was "a Gentile layman, not a preacher." Luke was an excellent medical practitioner with a very demanding schedule! Yet he found time (no, he *made* time) to "set forth in order" a "consecutive" account of our Lord's life, ministry, teachings, accomplishments, and assignment—**for one man**.

PERSISTENT REPRODUCTION

If you are to follow the New Testament standard, *you must do all that is humanly possible to procure persistent reproduction of disciples.* Every visionary disciple-maker must do all that is humanly possible, with full dependence upon God, to facilitate and perpetuate the reproduction of disciples. These disciples must clearly see the world as their field of operation, and must intentionally live to impact that world. Any visionary disciple knows that he cannot make anyone else see the standard or pursue the object without God's miracle power, but he also knows that unless he himself runs to the limit of his light in pursuing the standard, God will not cause anyone else to run with him. Augustine's rule holds, "Without God, we cannot; without us, God will not."

Luke has given us an unforgettable example of a consummate disciple-maker. He perfectly understood the importance of what he was doing. Luke made diligent inquiry into the life of Jesus of Nazareth, sought for perfect accuracy in his accounts, and knew the importance of a systematic order. Luke devoted himself to the task, assembled all available facts (written and oral) and wrote this document to *one lost man*—Theophilus.

What did Theophilus do with the document? He became so convinced of its truth that he received it fully, trusted the Person and message which it presented, and *sought to preserve it and pass it on to others.* Though this document was written to only one man, you hold a copy of it in your hand today! What an incredible example of the disciple-making, world-impacting standard of Jesus—a standard which He commands each of His followers to pursue. We call His command "the Great Commission.."

Luke won Theophilus to Jesus Christ by writing to him what we now call "the Gospel According to Luke." When Theophilus responded in personal faith in Christ, Luke immediately set out to disciple Theophilus *by writing another document, twenty-eight chapters in length*, which we call the Book of Acts, to introduce Theophilus to the world-impacting mandate and method of Jesus. What an *amazing and awesome example* of God's **word to flesh** standard! Remember that this standard was practiced by a layman who practiced medicine to pay the bills, but whose whole vocation was "turning people into disciples."

A pastor friend named Jim Davidson shared this illustration with me, which I shall quote in entirety:

My great, great grandfather Isaac Kilgore enlisted in the Confederate Army in 1862 at the age of eighteen. His first major battle was at Shiloh. To give you an idea of the fierceness of that battle, thereafter, whenever a soldier was describing how terrible a battle had been, he likely would say of it, 'I was more scared than I was at Shiloh.'

Ike went on to fight at Chickamauga, Chattanooga, Kennesaw Mountain, Atlanta, Franklin, and Nashville, to name a few. Awful fights. And for some of the time, he was the regimental color bearer. The color bearer was the man most likely to get shot, yet Ike survived even that. Over six hundred twenty thousand men died in the Civil War. ***Consider how that has effected the population today.***

After Ike mustered out at the end of the war, he walked from North Carolina to Walker County, Alabama, where he married twice and had seventeen children. ***Consider how that has effected the population of today!*** *And because he lived through the war, he reproduced multiplying generations of* *descendants. One of them is me, and I have two children, who likely will also have children. But what if Ike had died in the war?*

The key for you is this: If you receive the proper training as a good soldier must, and if you do not succumb in the war—and it is a war—you will reproduce persistently, generation upon generation, for Jesus Christ. But you must consider this as well: You will reproduce those generations for Jesus Christ ***only if you do die to self.*** *Jesus said, "Unless a kernel of wheat falls to the ground and dies, it remains only a single seed. But if it dies, it produces many seeds and many harvests."*

Will you assume personal responsibility for this, engage in painstaking research to accomplish it, develop and use precise resources to build New Testament disciples, and devote yourself to God to generate persistent reproduction through coming generations? Both God and the world of men are waiting for you![2]

---

[2]I express my deepest thanks to my dear Timothy/brother in Christ, Clint Davis, for his great work in transcribing a taped message to get this study ready for publication. Clint, may God graciously give you world impact for many generations!

Chapter 6
God's Multiplication Table

"And the things that thou hast heard of me among many witnesses, the same commit thou to faithful men, who shall be able to teach others also." *2 Timothy 2:2*

The great spiritual blast-off stimulated by the Day of Pentecost was underway. The early church was about to be propelled by the force of that blast-off to the ends of the world of its day. Peter had just concluded his sermon, explaining the Gospel of the Death and Resurrection of Jesus and the coming of the Holy Spirit; and verse 41 of Acts 2 says, "Then they that gladly received his word were baptized: and the same day there were added unto them about three thousand souls." Pretty prolific addition! No pastor on earth would be anything but elated over the conversion of 3000 people in one day after he had preached the Gospel. Give special note to the word "added." The same word recurs in verse 47 of the same chapter. Scan verses 42 through 47a, then hear this sentence: "And the Lord added to the church daily such as should be saved." Note again the word "added."

Now turn to Acts 5:14. The tragic story of the sin and judgment of Ananias and Sapphira has just been recorded. Verse 13 says, "And, the rest dared no man join himself to them: but the people magnified them." How would you like to belong to a church that is so spiritually powerful that people are actually afraid to join it? But verse 14 said, "And believers were the more added to the Lord, multitudes both of men and women." The "adding machine" has broken down! They can't number them any longer because so many are being added to the Lord.

Now notice a significant change. In chapter six, God's mathematical strategy of growth for the early church apparently accelerates. In verse one we read, "And in those days, when the number of the disciples was *multiplied*, there arose a murmuring of the Grecians against the Hebrews, because their widows were neglected in the daily ministration." The proper "M and M" order is "multiplied," "ministration," and "murmuring." When members multiply in a church, additional ministries must follow, both to provide for them and to employ them; and as surely as daylight follows darkness, murmuring will follow multiplication. It is part of the territory that more *people* will always mean more *problems*. After all, aren't you a problem of one kind or another?

Note the nature of the problem. A daily "deaconing" (the word translated "ministration") took place to distribute food, supplies, and money to the vast number of new Christians who had come under immediate economic stress and social ostracism because of their faith in Christ. The "Grecians" were Hellenized, Greek-speaking Jews who had been born outside of Israel and had recently returned for the Passover and Pentecost feasts. Some of them had come to Christ as a result of the Gospel events that had occurred dramatically in Jerusalem. The "Hebrews" were native-born Jews who spoke the Aramaic language of Palestinian Jews. The Grecians were the minority group, and the Hebrews were the vast majority group.

So the murmuring arose (reasonably) from the minority group as a protest against their widows being neglected in the daily distribution of goods. "The majority was taking care of itself to the abuse and neglect of the minority," they said. To take care of the problem, the Apostles appointed seven men, all with Greek-speaking names. This is sensible, isn't it? To solve the problem and stifle the protests, men from the ranks of the murmuring party were appointed to supervise the distribution of goods. The problem was solved, "and the word of God increased; and the number of the disciples MULTIPLIED in Jerusalem greatly; and a great company of the priests were obedient to the faith" (Acts 6:7). So massive was the multiplication that there was even a heavy leakage from the Jewish priesthood into the community of faith in Christ in Jerusalem. Note that multiplication is now the common standard for the growth of the early church.

In chapter 9, the acceleration continues. Chapter nine records the conversion story of the greatest of all Christians, Saul of Tarsus. When the turmoil over his conversion and early preaching had subsided, we read in verse 31, "Then had the churches rest throughout all Judea and Galilee and Samaria, and were edified; and walking in the fear of the Lord, and in the comfort of the Holy Ghost, were multiplied." Because the noun is so far removed from the verb in that sentence, it might be easy to miss the multiplication standard here. Now the *churches* are *multiplying*! Question: Whatever happened to that kind of Christianity? *They had no missionary societies, no committees or staff for church planting, no official home or foreign missionaries, yet the churches were multiplying.* Whatever happened to that kind of Christianity?

The answer may be fairly seen by attending almost any

pastors' conference in the United States today. When preachers begin to assemble, they ask several usual and universal questions. "Did you have a good day Sunday?" "Yes, we did." And what is the next question? "How many *additions* did you have?" Friends, it is not possible to impact a radically multiplying world population by merely having *additions* to our churches, *however many we may have.* The pace of multiplication cannot be matched by addition! Somebody has deceived us somewhere about something awfully important.

On the day Noah's ark landed after the flood, the animals were emerging from the ark in a spirit of great celebration. All, that is, except two—a pair of snakes. As they came out of the ark, they were weeping heartbrokenly. Noah said, "What's going on? Don't you know that this is the greatest day in world history? Why are you weeping while everyone else is celebrating?" One of the snakes sadly answered, "We're sad because you told us to multiply—and we're ADDERS!" That silly story points to a great tragedy in the Christian community. God has called us to multiply, and we have tragically reduced ourselves into mere adders. The magnitude of this tragedy cannot be measured.

We must not underestimate the value and importance of additions (conversions) to the Christian community, but we must force ourselves to face a tragic error in our procedures if the additions do not become catalysts for multiplication in the total Christian world community.

The only marching orders Jesus ever gave His church is called the Great Commission. There are seven verb forms in that Commission, but *only one of them is a command. There is only one strong imperative, only one command, in the Great Commission!* The verb is translated "teach" in the KJV, but it is again apparent that somebody is hiding something from us. The verb means much, much more than mere teaching! The verb means to "make disciples," or "turn men into disciples." We need to immediately stop asking, "How many *decisions* did you have?" and begin asking, "How many *disciples* are you building?"

The early church multiplied by using the standard and the procedure patterned perfectly in the three-year public ministry of Jesus with His twelve apostles. He was the original disciple-maker, and the procedure He followed must be examined, studied, mastered, and copied by us if we are to *reproduce reproducers* as He did. I personally do not believe an individual can be a *disciple* without also being a disciple-*maker*. Our obedience to His Lordship necessarily includes a priority in the fulfillment of His Great Commission. I believe disciple-making is built into the contract of being a disciple. If one is a New Testament disciple, he will necessarily be a disciple-maker.

THE PROFILE OF A MULTIPLYING DISCIPLE

Now turn to Second Timothy, chapter 2. In Second Timothy 2, we find seven great pictures of a disciple, and a great presentation of God's "multiplication table." First, the profile of a disciple. Each of the seven supplies a part of the portrait or picture of a New Testament disciple.

A "SON"

First, a New Testament disciple is a "son" (verse one). He is a son of God by a birth from above; but here, he is the spiritual son of the believer who led him to Christ. Paul called Timothy "my son," because he had led him to Christ. Paul had come to the town where Timothy lived on one of his missionary journeys. He found a family which included two great Old Testament students, a grandmother named Lois, and a mother named Eunice (II Timothy 1:5).

Eunice had a hybrid son (his father was a Greek) named Timothy. When Paul found how well-taught the boy was in the Bible, he easily led him to Christ. As he began to disciple him, he saw an apparent spiritual potential in the boy that was very exceptional. When Paul left to continue his missionary journey, he encouraged the boy to continue his walk with Jesus. Paul promised to pray for him daily, and also promised that he would return when possible.

Sometime later, on another missionary journey, Paul did return to Timothy's town. When he checked on the young boy, his fondest dreams were realized. The boy had grown beyond Paul's expectation spiritually. When Paul was ready to leave, he said, "Timothy, how would you like to make a trip with me?" Timothy was aghast. "Me? With you?" "Yes," Paul replied, "a trip with me." "What will we do?" "You watch me, pray for me, and we'll talk at night." When you are a visionary Christian, that is disciple-making!

What does a good son do? He learns from his parent, loves his parent, obeys his parent, and extends the family traits. And so does a spiritual son.

A "SOLDIER"

Second, a New Testament disciple is a "soldier." "Thou therefore endure hardness, as a good soldier of Jesus Christ. No man that warreth entangleth himself with the affairs of this life; that he may please him who hath chosen him to be a soldier." What does a good soldier do? He abandons all of his own plans and purposes to fulfill the duty assigned him. He trains with great discipline and effort. He defends the interest of his homeland. He fights when it is necessary. In short, he is ready for struggle and sacrifice, which are essential if he is to fulfill his assignment.

Captain beloved, battle wounds were Thine,
Let me not wonder if some hurts be mine.
Rather, O Lord, let my deep wonder be,
That I may share a battle wound with Thee.

AN "ATHLETE"

Third, a New Testament disciple is like an "athlete." Verse 5 says, "And if a man also strive for masteries [competes to win] yet is he not crowned, except he strive lawfully." It has been estimated that there are more than 50 references in the New Testament to athletics. What does a good athlete do? He applies himself totally to his sport, trains rigorously and steadily, masters the required skills, strives for mental discipline as well as physical, and does his best to excel. A Christian disciple will do no less in following Christ.

A "HUSBANDMAN"

Fourth, a New Testament disciple is pictured as a "husbandman," or a farmer (verse 6). What does a good farmer do? He labors, he breaks up the soil, he sows seed, he cultivates, and he reaps the crop. He also lays aside seed for future sowing, reaping and multiplying. All of these activities have evident counterparts in the spiritual exercise of being a disciple and making disciples.

A "WORKMAN"

Fifth, a New Testament disciple is a "workman" (verse 15), and a specialized workman at that. He is to be "a workman that needeth not to be ashamed, rightly dividing the word of truth." In order to do this, he must "study to shew himself approved unto God." As Christian disciples, we are here to labor and not to loaf.

A "VESSEL"

Sixth, a New Testament disciple is a "vessel" (verses 20-21). What is a vessel? A vessel is a hollow object intended to contain something or someone. As Christians, we are intended to contain and convey the very life of Christ Himself. What does a good vessel do? It sits on its master's shelf, empty and available, and waits for him to fill it if he wishes. The Christian disciple never has to wonder whether his Master wants to fill him or not. Ephesians 5:18 commands him to "be filled with the Spirit." When it is filled, it waits for him to pour it out. It simply waits for him to employ it as vessels are normally used. So should it be with a Christian disciple.

A "SERVANT"

Finally, a New Testament disciple is a "servant," or bond-slave (verse 24). A bond-slave has no will of his own, no schedule of his own, no rights of his own, and no property of his own. He is completely at his master's disposal. However, he is not lacking in resources. His master's checkbook endows any assignment the slave may receive. And so it is with a Christian disciple.

THE PROCEDURE FOR MULTIPLYING DISCIPLES

Now, having seen the profile of a disciple, as presented in II Timothy 2, let's examine the procedure for multiplying disciples. I call it "God's multiplication table." It is recorded in verse 2, where Paul said to Timothy, "And the things that thou hast heard of me among many witnesses, the same commit thou to faithful men, who shall be able to teach others also." Notice that there are four generations of disciples in this one verse: "Me . . . thou . . . faithful men . . . others also." The process of multiplication in this verse can be diagramed like this:

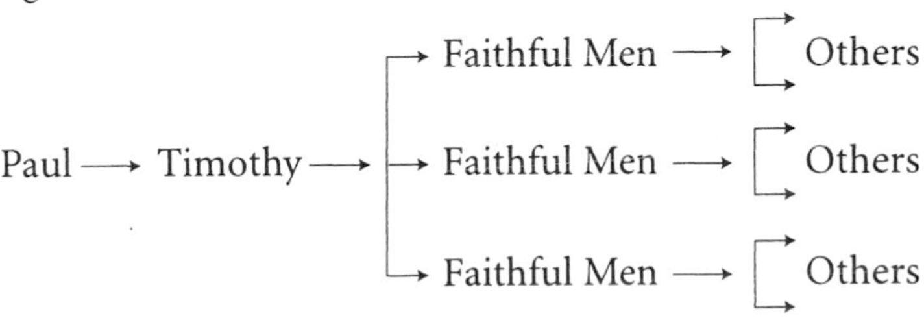

You get the impression that the process is like a widening funnel, with the little end being where Paul and Timothy stand. Everything begins with "me" and "thou," Paul and Timothy, and this association indicates two crucial things about disciple-making:

(1) The importance of the individual, and
(2) The importance of positive relationships.

Take away either of the two initial individuals, Paul or Timothy, and the process collapses at its inception. No multiplication can occur without a solid integer at the beginning—

and others to relate to.

Both Paul and Timothy must each be of a certain quality and commitment as disciples if multiplication is to happen. Then, they must be related to each other in a winsome, open, trustworthy way. How the church needs to extensively explore and apply relational theology! This is an entire universe that generally is hardly touched in the church at large. If Paul and Timothy had not had a relationship based on trust and availability, the chain would have broken as the first links were being forged. But, happily for us and all future generations, Paul was a winsome, attractive, disarming ambassador for Christ; and Timothy was an available, teachable, faithful disciple.

HOW DOES THE PROCESS REACH A DISCIPLE?

A question arises: How did Paul "get it across" to Timothy? How did the process reach Timothy? How did Paul's contagion spread to him so that he himself became contagious with it? Paul said, "The things that thou has *heard* of me...." Is it merely a matter of *hearing*? Is the curriculum merely academic concepts, or philosophical ideas, which may be classroom taught from one generation to the next? Hardly! What does "hearing" mean in the New Testament? Why is hearing singled out to picture spiritual intake instead of seeing, or smelling, or tasting, or touching? Indeed, there are spiritual counterparts to each of these physical senses. Then why is hearing singled out? Could it be because hearing is the sense by which objective reality goes *most directly* to the inner being? In every other sensory intake, a translation is necessary. Sight (visual images) must be translated to ideas and thoughts to reach the inner being. The same is true of touch, smell, and taste. But in hearing, the most direct communication occurs. So "faith comes by hearing, and hearing by the word (*hrema*, a vital, lovingly addressed word) of God."

WHAT DOES THE PROCESS OF HEARING ENTAIL?

In the process of disciple-making, just what does this all-inclusive "hearing" entail? Two verses in II Timothy 3 give us a clue (verses 10 and 11). Paul wrote, "Thou hast *fully known* (Paul lived a perfectly transparent life with Timothy; transparency . . . transmission . . . transformation, that's the order) my *doctrine* (teachings), *manner of life* (lifestyle), *purpose, faith* (actually, faithfulness or fidelity), *longsuffering* (ability to suffer a long time), *charity* (love), *patience, afflictions* (so Paul didn't hide the severity from Timothy)."

This is the natural outcome of what has been called the "with him" or the "with me" principle. Jesus "ordained twelve that they should be *with him*" (Mark 3:14). Being a disciple and making disciples are lifestyles that are *caught* more than they are *taught.* Can you imagine anybody making a lengthy trip with Paul and *not* being changed by it?

ONCE A DISCIPLE IS EQUIPPED, WHAT DOES HE DO?

Now, once Timothy has been "equipped," or "fully furnished," or "fully trained," what does he do? "The things that thou hast heard of me among many witnesses, the same commit thou to faithful men."

Two words call for special treatment in defining Timothy's role. He is to pass it on (the entire faith, lifestyle, and commitment) to "faithful" men. Great care must be taken here. This is one of the essential features of the genius of Christianity. When it functions properly, it *always guarantees* second and third-generation leadership. This is why it is absolutely essential that a discipler only seek to instill the process into *faithful* men. If his disciples prove to be unfaithful, the entire process stops with them, and all future generations may be left without skilled spiritual leadership.

The other word which calls for special attention is the dominant word in the verse. It is the word "commit." Again, great care must be given to understand this word. It is a banker's term. It literally means to "deposit." When you make a deposit in a savings account in a bank, you are hoping to gain a dividend, to draw interest. So it is when you make a disciple. You are not merely disinfecting a sinner. You are making a quantitative and qualitative investment that will accrue interest indefinitely into eternity.

AN INVESTMENT OR AN EXPENDITURE?

So, let me ask a crucial and sober question: Is your present life more of an *expenditure* or an *investment*? Are you *spending* it or *investing* it? Think carefully here. If you are *spending* it, the expenditure is *final*. There is no dividend from the act. Frankly, most "Christian activities" we engage in—whether church attendance, Bible reading, prayers, etc.—are expenditures more than they are investments. They are "survival" activities to make us "good Christians" instead of investments which will impact the world to the ends of the earth 'til the end of time. Thus, they betray the Commission of Jesus.

Timothy was to take the total investment of Christ's life that had passed from Paul to him and "deposit" it in turn in the lives of faithful men, and the process has not been properly passed on unless they are "able to teach others also." So, the process should be constantly enlarging into an expanding funnel that encompasses more and more territory and includes more and more people.

ILLUSTRATIONS TO SHOW THE IMPORTANCE AND THE POTENTIAL OF MULTIPLICATION

Let me employ some common illustrations to show both the importance and the potential of multiplication.

AN EVANGELIST

Suppose there was an evangelist who could (and did) win 1,000 persons per day to Christ (as converts). If the present population of the world were "frozen" so that nobody else is born and no one dies until the last person on earth is won to Christ, it would take over 15,000 years to win this present world population to Christ! And we must remember that they are only converts, not necessarily disciples.

A DAILY DAY OF PENTECOST

Or, suppose the day of Pentecost was reproduced daily, with 3,000 conversions every day. It would take approximately 5,000 years to win this present world population to Christ! And the population is hardly standing still! It is multiplying at a staggering rate. Seems pretty hopeless, doesn't it?

This is why we must implement the Bible standard of multiplication. This is a mechanical, hypothetical, theoretical illustration, but it will serve to let us see the possibilities of spiritual multiplication. If one discipler were thoroughly "infected" so that he could be an adequate trainer, and he were to enlist a disciple for a year of training which would enable him to enlist and train another the following year, and this were to go on, mechanically and consistently multiplying through the years, this process would pass the "1,000-a-day" evangelist at the beginning of the 23rd year; and would (hypothetically) *disciple* the entire population of the world in about 35 years. Note the difference between the "converts" of the evangelist and the "disciples" of the visionary reproducer.

A word of caution: such illustrations as this must not be used to play the activity of evangelists and soul-winners against the activity of disciple-makers. These are complementary roles, each absolutely essential. Indeed, it might even be hoped that both roles could be combined in each maturing believer.

DOUBLING OF PENNIES

Another familiar illustration: If I were to offer you one penny on the first day of a 31-day month, and offer to double the sum each day for 31 days (so that on the second day you have 2 cents, on the 3rd day 4 cents, on the 4th day 8 cents, etc., etc.); or offer you the outright sum of $1 million, which would you take? If you took the million dollars, you would be losing over 9.7 million dollars. But remember where it starts—with one penny. Without the invested first penny, the process never begins.

Why is disciple-making working so poorly? Frankly, God cannot find enough qualitative "first pennies." There are simply not enough visionary disciple-makers to begin the process world-wide. However, this must not discourage us. With vision and communication, this can be corrected much more rapidly than we might think. And remember, it is Paul to *Timothy*, a "second penny." The process largely depends on the quality, commitment, vision, and work of the first two pennies. Why? Because they are usually, at the beginning, the only models of this process their companions will ever see, as tragic as this may be.

So, penny number one and penny number two are all-important. But think for a moment all the way to the 31st day of the doubling process. On the last day, the sum goes from approximately 5.3 million dollars to approximately 10.6 million dollars. *So each day's multiplication is crucial to the finished result. No enlisted individual can afford to fail. If one Christian fails in the multiplication process, he cuts the potential for fulfilling the Great Commission in his lifetime exactly in half. However, if one Christian succeeds (multiplies), he doubles that potential in his lifetime.*

THE VISION OF WORLD IMPACT BY DISCIPLE-MAKING

Christian, do you have the vision of world impact by disciple-making? Are you qualitatively investing the Jesus-lifestyle, the Jesus-vision, and the Jesus-commitment in the lives of individuals so that they have a similar vision and commitment and can impart them to others? Someone has wisely said that in order to impart a vision to others, you yourself must:

- *See it clearly,*
- *Say it creatively*
- *Show it constantly*
- *Share it compassionately, and*
- *Safeguard it carefully.*

Stacy Kinehart wrote in his book, ***Living in the Light of Eternity***, "Some of us who came to Christ in the 1960's thought we would change the whole world in our generation. We had visions of great throngs of people, cup in hand, waiting patiently for us to dispense the Water of Life. The world has long since slid into an abysmal state. We have personally lowered our expectations to helping a moderate number of individuals over the course of a lifetime. But the real question, the one that rescues us from disillusionment and feelings of failure, is this: Is that really a lowering? Is it a small and insignificant vision unworthy of real sacrifice? Not when we consider the One who reached the world with a handful of men, who constantly multiplies His own life in people,whether or not we happen to be around to tabulate the 'results.'"

In fact, not only is "helping a moderate number of individuals" *not* a "lowering"; it is the only way one individual can qualitatively impact the world *to the ends of the earth until the end of time.*

Later in the same book, Mr. Rinehart says that "every Christian has the potential for an eternal impact in countless lives." However, some serious, almost embarrassing questions must be asked. Is our "fox" the same one Jesus went after—the whole wide world of people? Are we actually qualitatively and systematically investing in the lives of the individuals we work with to guarantee that we are closing in on that "fox"? Are we imparting the vision so that our disciples are consumed with it and thus will communicate it automatically to others?

Think your way through to the finished outcome of world impact and create your own sober questions to test the process. Disciple-making requires continued education, information, indoctrination, study, discussion, encouragement, accountability, and personal refinement.

Peter Wagner said, "The mission fields of the world are overloaded with evangelistic *programs that are not functioning properly. Sadder yet, many people deeply involved in them don't even realize the fact. In many of these programs,* believe it or not, *the results are not even tested.*" Friends, we cannot afford the luxury of the unexamined life or ministry.

Dietrich Bonhoeffer once boldly said, "A righteous person is one who lives for the next generation." Disciple-making, properly done, both forces and guarantees that kind of righteousness. Are you still thinking of occasional "additions" to the church, or are you a solid integer in God's multiplication table? Think carefully, because many generations may depend on you.

Chapter 7

The Genius of Jesus' Strategy

We will begin this chapter by "dropping in" on an innocent-sounding text. In fact, you might read Paul's First Thessalonian letter a hundred times and give little or no attention to this verse. But—and this is quite often the case in Scripture—God hides the genius of Heaven in seemingly "obscure" or inconspicuous texts, and here is a perfect case in point. Hidden away in this text is the glory and the genius of Christianity. The verse is I Thessalonians 3:8, which says (KJV), "For now we live, if ye stand fast in the Lord." Note that every word is a monosyllable, so this text is certainly very simple. But the glory of it is far out of proportion to its apparent simplicity.

Remember that the New Testament was originally written in the Greek language, and one advantageous feature of the Greek language is that the placement and arrangement of the words in a sentence reveals whether any of the words carry emphasis, and, if so, whether the emphasis is *minor* (the Holy Spirit raises His Voice) or *major* (the Holy Spirit *shouts*). In I Thessalonians 3:8, the words are so arranged that *one word carries* emphasis, and it is *major* emphasis (the Holy Spirit *shouts* this one word from the page to us). Again and again, I have asked audiences to *guess* which word they think the emphatic word is. Note that there are only eleven words in the entire verse, and yet the normal audience will go through *six* or *eight* guesses and still not be correct. You see, we cannot with our human minds guess right about God. Even if we stumble onto a correct answer, our answer is wrong in that it is still a *guess.* This is the reason we must study the Bible, "rightly dividing the Word of Truth" (II Timothy 2:15).

The one emphatic word (stressed with *major* emphasis) is the word *"ye."* Take a moment and read the verse aloud, and shout the word "ye." Can you now unravel the meaning? Can you now see the genius of Christianity? Can you see clearly why the word "ye" would be the emphatic word? Let's explore further until we have a firm grasp of this handle of understanding.

There are two lifestyles which human beings may pursue. Most human beings never realize this, but one of these patterns is *Satan's* lifestyle while the other is the *Savior's* lifestyle. One is the normal lifestyle of a *sinner* (and it is the *only* lifestyle a lost man may live), and the other is the normal lifestyle of a *practicing saint.* I use these words carefully, because any saved person may still at any time lapse into the practice of Satan's lifestyle.

Let me draw a simple diagram that will enable us to clearly see these contrasting lifestyles. I call this pattern the

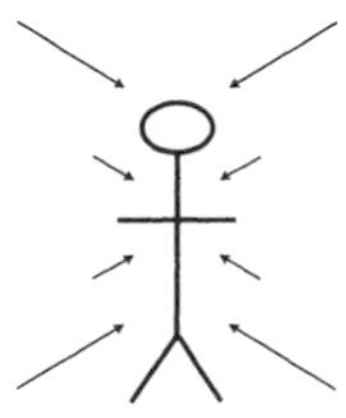

"outside-in" lifestyle. This is the inevitable, necessary lifestyle of every person who has never been born of God. He lives like a sponge, always sucking resources from his environment for his own selfish advantage. This is Satan's lifestyle. This is what created Satan: "I will," he repeated again and again, transferring his trust from God to himself. This is the classic definition of sin: "S-I-N," "Self-Ish-Ness." Sin is the "self-curl" of life which makes every human being turn everything back into himself. Sin is man's attempt to find meaning and fulfillment in life *for himself* and *in himself*—without God.

Now, the sad and tragic admission must be made that a born-again person may also revert back to this lifestyle. Because he carried the "flesh" into his new life in Christ (to understand the word "flesh," remove the letter "h" and reverse the letters: "self"), he may at any time trust himself and seek self-advantage instead of trusting Christ and living for God's glory. When a Christian lives selfishly, he falls into one of two categories. He falls into a course of "selfish" living, or into a course of "survival" living. Everything he does puts him into the discomfort of living for his own self-advantage or his own survival. Even if he reads the Bible, prays, and tries to serve God, he does it for some self-centered reason. The Bible calls this self-centered motive "carnal."

The other lifestyle may be seen in this diagram. The figure on the left represents Jesus, and the other figure repre-

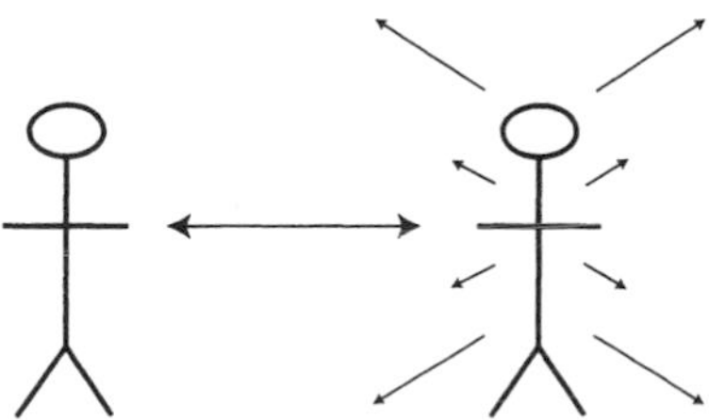

sents the born-again believer. The saved person has transferred his trust from self and self-effort to Christ. An interaction has occurred between him and Christ. Christ's life has entered into him and "the center of gravity" in him has shifted from self to Christ. This is called "salvation," "conversion," "regeneration," "the new birth," in the Biblical vocabulary of faith. All of these words depict *an absolute miracle of God which shakes a sinner at the very core of his being* and *"un-selfs" him, putting the glorious Lord Jesus Christ at the center of his life* instead of the old Satan-programmed self. I say again, this is an absolute miracle of God! Unsaved people will always misunderstand the new birth, reducing the term to a mild new beginning or dismissing it as a fanatical religious term. Could an unborn person possibly understand human life? What an absurd question!

The second diagram pictures what I call the "inside-out" lifestyle, the lifestyle of God. Jesus "gave Himself for us," expressing God's normal *modus operandi.* And the practicing Christian lives in a faith relationship with Jesus Christ, always receiving the remarkable resources of such a true life of true faith. These resources pass through him and satisfy him as they move out toward someone else.

Now read the verse again: "Now we live, if YE stand fast in the Lord." The typical Christian misunderstanding sounds like this: "I live if I pray enough." "I live (as a Christian) if I read the Bible enough." "I live if I am *committed* enough." "I live if I am *loyal* enough." "I live if I am *good* enough." "I live if I am *motivated* enough." "I live if I am *dedicated* enough." "I live if I am *effective* enough." But all of these good-faith statements have the subtle tendency to turn the individual's life back *upon* and *into himself* again. This is the subtle self-curl of the flesh, and it deceives many saved people.

Jesus said, "He who would save his own life (the self-advantaged, self-curled, survival life) shall lose it, but he who would give his life for My sake and the Gospel's shall save it." So the lifestyle pictured in the first diagram is a life of loss, but the self-forgetful, self-giving, self-disinterested lifestyle of the second diagram is the saved life.

Now change the figure just a bit. The same thing is true of *churches* that is true of *individuals.* Churches also may be

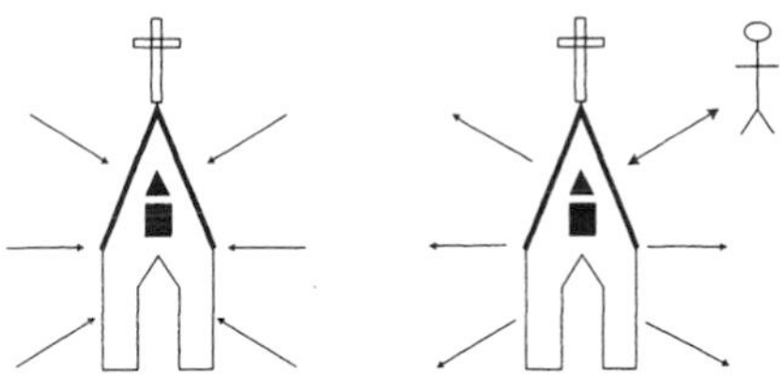

turned in on themselves, living *selfishly* or for their own *survival* (even while seeking people, the course may still be only one of *implosion!*), instead of extending and exhausting their supply lines in such a way that they constantly test and tax the miracle resources of God.

The Christian lifestyle is to live so *relationally*, so *unselfishly*, so *self-forgetfully*, so *other-orientedly*, that the individual Christian only truly lives *if his disciple is standing fast in the Lord.* Paul said, "I only *live* if *you* stand fast in the Lord." So the Christian lives *in, by means of, for,* and *through* his disciples!

Is this not Jesus' entire method, manner, and means of world impact? He so built Himself into twelve men that, after a three-year training period, he said, "Good-bye! Now My life is totally in your care. I only live if you stand fast!" That, dear friends, is what disciple-making is all about. How I wish I could explain this again and again, exploring its many facets like the facets of a bright and priceless diamond, until every reader was overwhelmed with the glory, the possibilities, and the vocation of this "inside-out" lifestyle.

Almost all Americans will recognize this familiar adage: "Practice makes Perfect." I was taught this as long as I can remember. It was expressed to me as if it were an invariable, invisible, infallible law. But I want to raise a serious question. Suppose the standard practiced is an *imperfect standard.* Can all the practice in the world ever "make perfect"? Certainly not! You see, practice only makes *permanent*; it does not necessarily make perfect. Now the application. Could it be possible that the church of Jesus Christ has so operated by traditional standards and understandings that all of its "practice" is only further setting it in an imperfect standard.

If the premise of these studies is correct, that the Great Commission presents the only "Marching Orders" Jesus Christ gave to His church, and if the understanding of the Commission presented in these studies is correct, then the typical strategy of the typical church is wrong. Has institution-building to a greater or lesser degree replaced individual-building in today's church? Remember that the interpretation of "turning people into disciples" is determined by the method and mandate of Jesus. His mandate is clearly stated in the one command of the Great Commission: "turn people into disciples." And His method is shown in His inter-networking small-group strategy with twelve men.

Let me ask the question again. Would the Christianity presently represented in your church have produced the Book of Acts to begin with? This is an embarrassing question, and thus it will not receive a ready answer. To put it another way:

would the Christianity of the Book of Acts tolerate the world situation of today, a situation in which nearly half of the human race remains unevangelized (2,000 years after Christ!), and in which 4/5 of the human race are (at best) only poorly evangelized? Would the Christianity of the Book of Acts tolerate the situation in the church in almost every evangelized country of the world, a situation which is described with monotonous refrain in Patrick Johnstone's ***Operation World***: "This country suffers from a desperate lack of trained leaders"? The embarrassing answer to all of the above questions is a resounding "No!" Then, will the present strategies and methods correct these failures? Well, they have not succeeded as of this writing. Should we not back away, boldly re-examine the original strategy of Jesus, and see what variations have carried us away from His strategy?

There is a common term used in the church, another of those church terms which we have superficially presumed upon. It is the term, "Christ-like." Almost all Christians would admit that the goal of the Christian life is to make the individual believer Christ-like. In fact, this is God's clearly-stated goal for each of His children. Romans 8:29 indicates that it has always been God's purpose to "conform us to the image of His Son," or to make us like Christ. But again, we have stopped far short of the Biblical mark in defining this term. We define it typically in terms of "the fruit of the Spirit" of Galatians 5:22-23. Who could fault this definition? If a person bears the fruit of the Spirit, his inner character is like that of Christ. But follow the analogy of fruit a bit further. Does fruit only have an *inner essence*, or does it also have an *outward form*? To illustrate, when a shopper goes to the supermarket to buy lemons, does she look for "lemonness"? No, she looks for a small fruit that has a small round shape, a yellow, thick skin, and a rough surface. In other words, a lemon has a clearly distinguishable outward form, conspicuously different from the outward form of a plum, a strawberry, or a cantaloupe. I suggest that the fruit of the Spirit is only a good *beginning* in defining Christians. *Does Christ-likeness have an outward form as well as an inner essence?*

Let me put it in one sentence: *you will never do anything more Christ-like than the training of groups of people to live in union with Jesus Christ inwardly, and to reproduce, multiply, and impact the whole wide world outwardly.* The basic strategy words are "training," (with the strategy and curriculum patterned by Jesus), "groups" (with the approximate size of each group again patterned by Jesus), "union" (thus making Christ's life, ministry and motivation ours), "reproduce and multiply" (the responsibility of every single child of God), and "impact the whole wide world" (which should provide the moment-by-moment goal of every single child of God). And all of this is to determine the strategies by which we accomplish the goal.

In John 19:30, in history's holiest moment, Jesus spoke the one word which is probably the most important single word ever spoken. The word is *tetelestai*, "finished," "complete," "done." The work that was finished at that moment is the work of *redemption*, the one inclusive word which describes all that God has done to fully save sinners.

In John 17:4, Jesus used that word again (KJV): "I have glorified Thee on the earth: I have finished the work which Thou gavest me to do." What work had Jesus *finished* at this point? Most commentaries say that this statement also applies to the work of redemption which Jesus accomplished on the cross, but this clearly cannot be the case. Jesus used a past-tense verb, and the cross was still in front of Him! No, He was not speaking here of the work of *redemption*, but the work of *reproduction*. At this point, His entire training process for His men was complete. So Jesus came to accomplish two primary and essential works: *redemption* and *reproduction*. Without the indispensable work of *redemption* accomplished by Christ's death on the cross, there would have been nothing worth reproducing, but without the indispensable work of *reproduction* through enlarging numbers of Christians, the work of *redemption* would be only partially, poorly, or pitifully known (the exact situation of today's world, and even of today's church, as well).

Again a crucial question is forced upon us. What does "reproduction" mean from a New Testament standpoint? How many people are expected to reproduce, and how much reproduction is to be expected of them? Is the reproduction mere duplication (the standard of soul-winning, or converting sinners to Christ), or is it to produce multiplication? If multiplication, on how large a scale? And how are valid goals in these categories to be reached? Again, the method and manner of Jesus are to provide our model.

Let's take one model for a momentary examination. What model did Jesus follow in reproducing? How did He produce multipliers? How did He produce a mind-set in twelve men that eventuated in massive world impact to the farthest reaches of the known world of His day within 60 years after His death? Read the last sentence again and let its truth saturate your mind. Let its question stir your heart. How? How *did* He . . . ? "How did he *produce a mind-set*? In twelve men!!?? That eventuated in massive world impact? To the farthest reaches of the known world of His day? And within 60 years after His death? He didn't have television, telethons, telephones, telecommunication means—just tell-a-person! How? How? How? Negatively, nothing of His program depended on a crowd. Nothing of His program depended on preaching (though He used mass communication to minister, to teach, and to emerge potential disciples). Nothing of His program was institutionalized (this is a mere admission of fact, not an evaluation of institutionalism). Nothing of His program centered in going to church (although He went to church regularly). **Then WHAT WAS HIS STRATEGY? HIS TECHNIQUE? HIS METHOD?**

We can get a hint by examining the Biblical lists of the men whom He called "apostles." Let it be said first that He trained them *to send them away from Him*, not to centralize increasing masses where He was. This strategy is conspicuously unlike today's church, which tends to evaluate its success (and the success of its leaders) almost totally by the measurement of size. The four lists of the Apostles are found in Matthew 10, Mark 3, Luke 6, and Acts 1. The compiling of the lists should stimulate ceaseless study. There are incalculable and eternal lessons to be learned from studying these lists over and over again. Let me place them on the page:

Matthew	*Mark*	*Luke*	*Acts*
Simon (called Peter)	Simon (named Peter)	Simon (named Peter)	Peter
Andrew	James, son of Zebedee	Andrew	John
James, son of Zebedee	John	James	James
John	Andrew	John	Andrew
Philip	Philip	Philip	Philip
Bartholomew	Bartholomew	Bartholomew	Thomas
Thomas	Matthew	Matthew	Bartholomew
Matthew	Thomas	Thomas	Matthew
James, son of Alphaeus	James, son of Alphaeus	James, son of Alphaeus	James, son of Alphaeus
Thaddaeus	Thaddaeus	Simon the Zealot	Simon the Zealot
Simon the Zealot	Simon the Zealot	Judas, son of James	Judas, son of James
Judas Iscariot	Judas Iscariot	Judas Iscariot	---

Note the most obvious features. The same name comes first on each list. Let me correct myself. It is the same *person*, though the name is not the same throughout ("Simon Peter" and then "Peter"). Let me correct myself again. He is the same person throughout—and yet he is clearly *not the same person*! The trip from "Simon" in control to "Peter" in control is a colossal study of the strategy, technique, method, and process of Jesus in building disciples. Was that (building disciples) not the only command in His Great Commission to us? Surely, then, the strategy, technique, method and process of Jesus are to be followed as nearly as possible by us (or we can fully expect a different product, which is precisely what has sadly occurred in today's church). It is an unbelievably rewarding study to trace just the training process Jesus followed with Simon Peter alone. If the passages of encounter, exchange and instruction between Jesus and Peter are to be the standard for building disciples in today's church, then it is very easy to see why we are suffering from a gigantic crisis of product (unbuilt Christians and a largely unevangelized world). I would recommend this study to any Christian. To examine the process by which Jesus reduced "Simon" (his pre-conversion, fleshly name) and emerged "Peter" (the name that is normally used for him in the Book of Acts) is an eye-opener for anyone wishing to know Jesus' technique in building disciples.

When you examine the second line across the lists, you see that the names are *not* the same. The same is true in the *third* line, and the *fourth*. But *eureka*, line number five contains the same name all the way across. This will prove to be crucial in understanding the training strategy of Jesus. Line six does not contain the same name, nor does line seven, nor does line eight. But *aha*! *Eureka, again!* Line number nine contains the same name all the way across. Line ten contains different names, so does line eleven, and line twelve (if you fill in the place vacated by the death of Judas Iscariot with the name of his selected replacement, Matthias).

We may now be seeing a primary technique employed by Jesus in building world-visionary, world impacting, reproducing multipliers of *others in kind.* We know without any doubt that Jesus' strategy was totally centered in a small group of twelve men. We know, too, that Jesus put all of His "eggs" in that one small "basket." His total plan for world impact was placed in the hands (and the productivity) of twelve men! And the lists of the Apostles also strongly suggest his method in building these men. He apparently (and it is far more apparent than a *first glance* will see) divided His twelve men into three equal groups of four each, with an assigned leader for each group. What evidence do we have for believing this? The evidence is too overwhelming to be mere coincidence. All the men in the first group (and only these, as far as we know) were followers of John the Baptist who came to follow Jesus upon the selfless encouragement of their leader. All the men in the first group are dynamic and impulsive men, just like their leader, Simon Peter. James and John were nicknamed "Sons of Thunder" by Jesus Himself! They were dispositionally like developing thunderstorms. Andrew is apparently far more dynamic than we normally think. After all, he was the first home missionary (John 1:40-42), the first youth worker and social worker (John 6:8-9), and the first foreign missionary (John 12:20-22). It is very unlikely that a timid man would have accomplished any of the things attributed in those passages! These were dynamic men.

The second group is headed by the Apostle Philip, who has throughout the Gospel the profile of a highly *philosophical* man. And every person in his group is also highly philosophical, men like "doubting" Thomas and Levi Matthew, who wrote the Gospel of the philosophical teachings of Jesus. Notice that Jesus did not install a philosophical man as his primary leader—He would have never accomplished anything! Philosophical men make great doubters, great questioners, great investigators, great protestors, great procrastinators, and finally, great contributors to the Christian mission. But out-front leadership was not given to philosophical men. However, we are not to under-estimate the importance and necessity of these men in evaluating this statement. It just reflects another important factor in the strategy of Jesus.

The third group—are you ready? The third group is made up totally of political revolutionaries! The leader, James, the son of Alphaeus, was probably the mildest one in the group! Judas' surname, "Iscariot," may well derive from the "sicarii," the little dagger carried by certain revolutionaries, with which they had pledged themselves to kill any Roman official whom they could reach in a crowd (or *anywhere*, for that matter). Here is an interesting feature. There is substantial evidence that James and Matthew (both called "sons of Alphaeus") were brothers. Does this stimulate great thought in you? Why was one (Matthew) a traitor to Rome, having given his life to exacting taxes from the Jews for the despised Roman government? Why was the other (James) an ardent Jewish patriot? Did one react against the other's extreme views and actions? Did James' patriotism drive Matthew toward Rome? Or did Matthew's defection drive James into ardent political and revolutionary action? Or neither? Any argument we may give is weakened by Scriptural silence, but the question surely arouses speculation. The man who is called "the Zealot" is named by his identification with the furiously patriotic, rebellious, and violent political party bearing that name. Did you know that, if Simon the Zealot had met Matthew the publican under "normal" circumstances, he would have killed him as quickly as possible. Do you see why I believe that Jesus' Greatest Miracle was not feeding the hungry by multiplying food, or healing sick people, or even raising the dead. To me, His Greatest Miracle was the construction—out of "impossible" material—of a band of Twelve Men who would send the shock waves of Spiritual Reproduction to the ends of the earth of that day! And, had not the church replaced the strategy of Jesus (building individuals . . .) with a suitable substitute that surely originated from another source (building imploding institutions), those shock waves would be impacting the ends of the earth today, and would continue to do so unabated until the end of time.

When the famed comedian, Charlie Chaplin, was alive, a "Charlie Chaplin Look-alike Contest" was held in Monaco. Mr. Chaplin traveled to the site, entered the contest anonymously—and came in *third*! I seriously wonder where the real Jesus would "place" in a Christ Look-alike Contest in *today's* church???

Do not misunderstand this chapter. There is no clear command which necessitates our following the exact group form. However, wisdom would suggest that "Christ-like" means "Christ-like." That sounds simple enough, but its truth has proved to be very elusive in the church. The *size* of Jesus' group appears very wise, as well as the divisions, affording accountability, assignments, fellowship, etc. But surely these were not closed and rigid groups. The outcome proves that Jesus was the Master of inter-networking group dynamics. Would we not be wise to do the same? Are we *really* wise if we *don't*?

I repeat: you . . . you . . . and you . . . and you . . . will never do *anything more Christ-like* in *all your life* than the training of individuals by the strategy of Jesus ("turn people into disciples") for *total world impact.*

Isn't it time we checked all our activity to be sure we are fulfilling solidly, fully, and consistently, the Commission of Jesus?

Chapter 8
How This Standard Works in a Church

"But unto every one of us is given grace according to the measure of the gift of Christ. Wherefore he saith, when he ascended up on high, led captivity captive, and gave gifts unto men. (Now that he ascended, what is it but that he also descended first into the lower parts of the earth? He that descended is the same also that ascended up far above all heavens, that he might fill all things.) And he gave some, apostles; and some, prophets; and some, evangelists; and some, pastors and teachers; For the perfecting of the saints, for the work of the ministry, for the edifying of the body of Christ: Till we all come in the unity of the faith, and of the knowledge of the Son of God, unto a perfect man, unto the measure of the stature of the fullness of Christ: That we henceforth be no more children, tossed to and fro, and carried about with every wind of doctrine, by the slight of men, and cunning craftiness, whereby they lie in wait to deceive."

Ephesians 4:7-14

Would the Christianity presently represented in your church have produced the Book of Acts to *begin* with? This is a stern and searching question. Honesty allows only one answer: No. Then what is the difference between the

Christianity that *did* produce the Book of Acts and the peculiar and distorted version that we see almost universally in the American church?

In the early church, they followed Jesus' model in *building people who count*, but today *we count people* in crowds. We tend to measure success almost totally in terms of size. Furthermore, our model is more one of *disinfecting sinners* for a *clean* life; theirs was more a model of *discipling saints* for *world impact*, though it certainly did not depreciate in any way a clean life. Our practice is more like putting converts into a safety deposit box called "eternal security" rather than each believer investing his total life into other saved individuals for the production of world-visionary, world-impacting reproducers of *other* world-visionary, world-impacting reproducers …

So what is the difference between the Christianity of 42 A.D. and the Christianity of 2,000 A.D.? Is Jesus different? No, we worship and serve the same Jesus they knew. Is the Holy Spirit different? No, the Holy Spirit I relate to today is the same Holy Spirit who "came" in the full release of redemptive power on the Day of Pentecost. Is the Bible different? Be very careful with this question, because the answer is "yes." *They* did *not have* a complete Bible. They were finishing the writing of the Bible through the activities recorded in the Book of Acts. So the advantage of the complete Bible lies in *our* court, *not* in *theirs*. Was the difference in technological or travel advantages? The very suggestion is ridiculous. We have *every* advantage; *they* had no logistical advantage. God had arranged the universal peace of the world by Roman might, and the worldwide network of Roman roads, but these were only slight advantages compared to ours today. They didn't have television, telephone, telegraph, telethon—they just had "tell-a-person." They did not have the "facs" but they had the FACTS! But so do we! Then, what accounted for the fact that *they* had impacted the entire known world in an incredibly short time, while today roughly two-fifths of the human race is totally unevangelized, and two-fifths more is very poorly evangelized. The remaining one-fifth has far more man-power and fire-power than that possessed by the early church, but to what result? Is the difference between us and them one of commitment? Some would argue long and loud that this is the difference, but it isn't. Not many people in the early church were any more committed than the typical Christian of today who faithfully attends church three times a week as well as special occasions— but still has almost no influence on the 2.3 billion people who have not heard of Christ. The Christianity of the Book of Acts would never tolerate such a statistic, but today's church can continue in all of its activities and pay almost no attention to the most tragic failure on earth.

So what is the difference between the Christianity of Alexander, Rufus, Tryphena, and Andronicus of the first century and Joe, Susan, Sam and Eddie of the twentieth century? *I* say that the difference is solely, exclusively, totally and alone one of *strategy. They* operated by a radically different strategy than we do!

Let me illustrate the *traditional institutional model* of today's American church. Picture a *bus* which travels to a destination and transports passengers along the way. The church is like the bus. The pastor is like the *bus driver.* The bus driver (pastor) welcomes the passengers on board (and they may be welcomed by their fellow passengers as well), they are *seated* and only arise to see to other necessary duties, and the bus driver (pastor) gives lectures on the scenery along the way as he drives the large numbers of passive, observing (possibly *sleeping*) passengers to their agreed destination. The typical passenger *endures* the ride, but he *never recruits another rider*, and *seldom testifies of his appreciation for the bus, the bus company, the route, or the trip.* In short, the achievement of the journey rests in the capability and efficiency of the bus and the performance of the driver. This is a far, far cry from the Christianity of Jesus and the early disciples. The Christianity of the Book of Acts was essentially a *people's* movement (Acts 1:8, Acts 8:1 and 4) and *not* a *preacher's* movement or an *institutionalized* movement.

At the North Pole there is a huge cap of ice on which the snow keeps building up. Scientists tell us that if it were ever to *melt* much of the world would be covered with water. Laymen might be called "God's frozen assets." If they were all melted before God and warmed to *His vision, His purpose, His goal, His strategy*, "the earth would be filled with the knowledge of the Lord, as the waters cover the sea."

God's model for his Church is clearly declared in Ephesians 4:7-14. The general subject of the passage is spiritual gifts, but the gifts dealt with here are not the normal variety of gifts presented in The New Testament. The lists of gifts in Romans 12, I Corinthians 12 and 14, and I Peter 4 are generally quite different. *Those* gifts are endowments from heaven placed by the Holy Spirit within believers. The gifts *here* are actually *gifted leaders* which the Holy Spirit gives to his Church for special, at-large purposes in the church, and for the accomplishment of special goals.

Let me give an outline which will supply an overlook of the entire passage (Ephesians 4:7-4). This passage focuses on the giver of the gifts, the gifts (gifted men), and the goals for which the gifts are given.

THE GIVER OF THE GIFTS

I. The Giver of these Gifts is Presented, verses 8-10

Three great facts are given about Jesus:

A. He descended, verses 9, 10.

B. He ascended, verses 8, 9, 10.

C. He transcends, verse 10B.

II. The Gifts (Gifted Men) are Profiled, verse 11

Four (possibly five) gifted leaders are mentioned:

A. "Apostles."

B. "Prophets."

C. "Evangelists."

D. "Pastor-teachers."

III. The Goals for Giving These Gifts are Proclaimed, verses 12, 13

A. To enlist members for the Body, verse 12b.

B. To equip members within the Body, verse 12a.

C. To employ members through and beyond the Body, verses 12-16.

Under "the Giver of the Gifts," which contains one of the great Christological (doctrine of the Person of Christ) passages in the New Testament, note one rule that emerges. Though Satan's way *down is up*, God's way *up is down*. "He who exalts himself (like Satan) will be abased (brought down to the basement of the universe), but he who humbles himself (like Jesus) will be exalted (like Jesus)."

The list of gifted men (verse 11) would provide the material for limitless study and speculation. For example, the question of the first two gifts mentioned is, do they exist in *today's* church? The "apostle" as an official position could only exist in the early church because the specific qualifications (seeing Jesus and being with Him) cannot be met by anyone after the first century. The office of "prophet" seems to be a distinctive *Old Testament* office. Also, Ephesians 2:20 speaks of apostles and prophets as the "foundation" of the church. Today, we are far up in the building of the superstructure. The foundation is important, but only *in its place*, *not* in the superstructure.

However, unprofitable speculation may cause us to miss the main point. The rule has often been stated, "like leader like follower." The follower will be like his leader (Luke 6:40, the words of Jesus). So when Jesus gave to His Church four leaders with distinct and distinguishable gifts, *He is clearly telling us what He intends His entire Church to be.*

APOSTLE

The word "apostle" means *"one sent away from,"* so he intends *His entire church* (! ! ! !) to be a *going* and *sending* fellowship. Many take refuge from the responsibility to go in the idea of *sending*, but this cannot be justified in the New Testament. Today's church? It is filled with *coming* people—people whose Christianity is defined by the faithfulness by which they *come* and serve. The very word "apostle" tells us why Jesus *chose* them (Ephesians 1:3, Acts 1:3). The word "chose" is a middle voice verb, meaning that Jesus chose them "for Himself," not primarily for their growth, their health, their wealth, their happiness, even *their* fulfillment. A misplaced emphasis has created a "consumer-friendly" Christianity, which is a radical misreading of the New Testament. The New Testament presents God *as* the *consumer*, and *we* are His fuel. Jim Elliott prayed truly, "Make me thy fuel, O flame of God!" What did Jesus choose us for? To *go* where *He* wants us to go— *"away from,"* not *"to"*—to be, say, and do *whatever He wishes.* So the only proper goal for any Christian must include a strategy to impact the very ends of the earth. Can we possibly see any proper limits on such a strategy in the Book of Acts? Oh, they tried to limit it to local, introverted attention, but *God* sent a *persecution* that scattered them like seeds (the very word that is used in Acts 8:1, and Acts 8:4, and in I Peter 1:1) *out* and *out* and *out* through the mixed soil of the Roman Empire. Be wary, Christian, because a giant latter-day persecution is closing in fast on the American Church. Violent fundamentalist Islam is storming the world, and only the poor and weak church of Jesus Christ is in its path. The technological achievements and blasphemous atheism of science and humanism have made potential persecutors everywhere. So the days of Christianity in its comfortable, convenient, fortress mentality are numbered. Another dispersion, or scattering of Christians, is on the way. And God is the Sower! You see, though we are conveniently hard of hearing about the responsibility to go, God is very serious about it.

PROPHET

The word "prophet" means a "forth-teller" (not primarily a "foreteller" of truth). A prophet is a *truth sayer* not a *soothsayer.* A prophet was a "herald," a "proclaimer," a "testifier." So when Jesus gave gifted prophets to His Church, He is showing that He intended His Church to be a non-stop, always faithful, always bold, always speaking, fellowship of people. "Let the redeemed of the Lord say so." This accomplishes several Divine purposes. It matures the speaker, because any person will pursue his spoken confession, whatever the confession is. It glorifies God, because He dwells in the praise and testimony of His people. And, it presents the Gospel to every listener. Never should any Christian check the temperature or pulse of the world before he speaks—else he never speak at all! We are speaking first *to* God, and *about* God, and *for* God, and therefore we must not be silent. "I believe, therefore have I spoken." The prophets, preachers, teachers, and leaders of the church must speak fully, clearly and boldly—and all believers must do the same.

EVANGELIST

The word "evangelist" means a "good newser," one who "good newses" Jesus to people, and people to Jesus. The Gospel admits some very bad news concerning Satan and his evil devices, man and his sinful condition and practice, God and His holy reaction against sin, and hell as the final asylum of the hopelessly inverted sinner. But sadly, the church has proclaimed the *bad* news far more often and far more forcefully than it has proclaimed the Good News. The great and dominant message of Scripture is called the "Gospel," *euaggelion*, the "Good News." Nobody has truly received the good news until he feels good about *God*, about *Jesus*, about the *Holy Spirit*, about *himself*, about his *salvation*, about his *present destiny and final destination*, and about the *ultimate outcome* of all things. God intends His Church to be glorious and victorious in its presentation of good news.

PASTOR-TEACHER

Then the word "pastor-teacher" yields a final truth of what God expects of His Church. The word "pastor" means "shepherd," and it tells us that He intends His people to *lead.* In order to lead, the Christian must clearly and confidently know *who he is, what he has, where he is going, how to get there, what his purpose is today and every day, and how to accomplish his assignment.* Any person who knows these things clearly and confidently can lead anyone. The word "teacher" indicates that Jesus intends His Church to be a truth-telling, educational, feeding fellowship. And this is the assignment of every believer. "By all means" (I Corinthians 9:22)—spontaneous word, prepared testimony, formal teaching and preaching, the dissemination of tracts, books, magazines, letters (God is *high* on letters), cassette and video tapes, radio and television, face-to-face and at a distance—the Christian's goal should be to influence, to bend, to sway, "to win some."

These are the "gifts" that are profiled; thus, the assignment, responsibility and pattern of the church may be clearly seen.

THE GOALS FOR THE GIVING OF THESE GIFTS

TO ENLIST MEMBERS

We are to "build up" the Body of Christ by the use of these gifted men and their emerging followers. So a new standard of enlistment must be immediately employed by the church. The full terms of enlistment must be immediately employed by the church. The full terms of the Christian "contract" must be stated and accepted from the first moment of decision—self-denial, cross-bearing (these are "front-door" requirements, not maturity additions), inside-out living, devotional and vocational Bible study, worship and warfare prayer, etc., etc. And these cannot be instilled as lifestyle by a 1-, 2-, or 3-hour-a-week exposure.

Where, in our evangelism, is a standard and practice for rejecting and dismissing the idolatrous rich young ruler? This devastating standard was employed by Jesus in dismissing a polite, orthodox, earnest, seeking inquirer (read Matthew

19:16-26 carefully). Incidentally, the young man's question, "What good thing shall I do, that I may have eternal life?" was actually asked *twice* of Jesus. A lawyer ("expert" on Moses' law) asked it in Luke 10:25 in another setting altogether. And neither time did Jesus give what most of us would consider an "orthodox, plan-of-salvation" answer. He applied the "mid-way test" at the *front door*!

You see, the word "believe," which is simplistically used by us to state the way of salvation, is itself a compound of two words, "by life," and it means "to *live* by." What you *behave* is what you *believe*! All the rest is airy talk, "much ado about nothing," pious words, often "full of sound and fury, but signifying nothing." This is the Christianity which *discusses* but never *does*, *"glories"* but never *goes*, *"delights"* but *disobeys*, *purges itself* for the sake of *cleanliness* but never *pours itself out* for the sake of *conquest*, *pours in* to fill the church (on Sunday morning) but never *pours out* to fill and impact the farthest reaches of the earth.... We must clearly state as an entrance requirement that the New Birth (which is performed and proscribed only by God) is necessarily followed by the New Life (which is equally produced and proscribed by God). So we need a new enlistment in today's church, an enlistment which understands the full revelation of Jesus. After all, should not a signee read and understand the entire contract before he "signs on the dotted line"?

TO EQUIP THE MEMBERS

Then, every member is to be "equipped" for his individual "work of ministering" (4:12a). This sentence contains one of the most expansive and definitive words of the New Testament. It is translated "perfecting" in the KJV, but (as usual) no single translation can possibly convey the full meaning of this word to us. One translation says that the gifted men are given to the church to "equip" its members; another says, "to fully furnish"; another, to "outfit" the members. One thing is certain: *all Christians—without exemption, exception, or exclusion*—are to be so equipped, or outfitted, or furnished. The introverted institutional model of today's church is that the pastor is the star on center stage, while the "laity" are left with odd jobs as stage hands, lighting technicians, and custodians. This model must be altered so that the pastor becomes the "outfitter" and the people the ministers. The clearly stated purpose of the outfitting is that each Christian may engage in "the work of ministering." You see, the day you were saved, *you were called into the ministry!* Your pastor is not any more of a minister than *you* are! In fact, you are to minister; your pastor is to equip you for the ministry. You see, we need to rid the world of *laymen* and *put every Christian into the full-time, vocational, going, proclaiming, good-newsing, leading and feeding ministry!* What a singing, shouting, overcoming, marching, penetrating, victorious army the church would be! Eugenia Price said, "The greatest sin of today's church is that it has almost totally tamed the Lion of Judah." We have tamed all the risk, all the threat, all the danger, all the martyrdom out of Christianity, so more interest, challenge, and excitement can be generated by a sports event or a rock concert than by the "all banners flying" march of the Church of Jesus Christ.

The word "equipped" is a cosmopolitan word. A study of the use of the word in the New Testament would both exhaust and shock us. In Greek, the basic word is *"katartismon."* The "kat" part is a prefix, and the "mon" part is an ending. Strip these away and you will get to the heart and the basic meaning of the word translated "equip" or "outfit" or "furnish" or "prepare for action." The root form is "artis"—from which we get our word "artisan." Eureka! The word "artisan" means a "skilled craftsman." Eureka!! The business of the pastor-teacher is to turn *every believer* of his constituency into *an absolute skilled craftsman in handling, understanding, living by, being dominated by, ministering with, etc., the Word of God.* This assignment consumed Jesus *as a strategy for Twelve Men* in hands-on, close-up, round-the-clock, on-the job training for approximately three years. Again, what does the word "Christlike" mean? If we cut away His Strategy, and omit His Great Commission, and disregard His Model, why should we bemoan the condition of the church and the world? We are only living with the commodity we produced. Remember that Perception leads to Process, and Process leads to Product. If the Product is wrong (and who can deny that it often *is*), then the *Proces*s must be wrong.

Look again at the word "equip." Research reveals that it was a widely used word in the Greek speaking world of the first century. And it carried many shades of meaning:

(1) To pacify a city that was torn by faction.
(2) To set a limb that has been dislocated.
(3) To develop certain parts of the body by exercise.
(4) To restore a person to his right mind.
(5) To reconcile friends who have been estranged.
(6) To fully furnish something or someone for a given purpose.
(7) To order things properly, or to correctly arrange things.
(8) To put something on the path of progress.

Before you leave this list too hurriedly, look back over it and translate each statement into the job description of the leaders of the Body of Christ. Then, translate each statement into the life and conduct of all the followers, because disciples will become like their teacher (Luke 6:40).

TO EMPLOY THE MEMBERS

So the traditional roles of "clergy" and "laity" must be reversed. The "laity" become the troops in the front lines (fully armed, fully aware, and fully active), and the "clergy," with the gathered church, exist to support them. Charles Colson was right when he wrote, "each of us as believers must see ourselves as ministers of the Gospel. We don't simply attend church, consuming a religious product." The Christian who has no personal ministry which eventuates into powerful world impact is a *distorted version* of a Christian. The goal is the full-time employment of every Christian in living the Christian life and penetrating and impacting the world by means of the strategy of Jesus. Again, the building of world-visionary, world-impacting multipliers emerges as the Top Priority (as in the Great Commission). In order for the church to correct its tragic distortions, it must practice a new and different *recruitment*, a new and different *equipment*, and a new and different *deployment*. May God open the eyes of our hearts and flood them with light (Ephesians 1:17-19)!

So the immediate purpose inside a fellowship of believers is to "equip the saints." This will require a full-orbed, all-cylinders-functioning training of every believer. The ultimate purpose is to "build up the church"—*qualitatively*, by *edifying* it on the *inside*, and *quantitatively*, by *enlarging* it from the *outside*. How far outside? *Each church* must see its assignment as *"the uttermost part of the earth."* So it must extend its "supply lines"—its personnel, its finances, its plans, strategies, and actions—to the very ends of the earth. Remember, the light that shines farthest shines brightest *at home*.

MODELS OF A LOCAL FELLOWSHIP OF BELIEVERS

Let me conclude this study by diagraming two models of a local fellowship of believers. One is the usual model in the American church, the other is the practical model called for in our text.

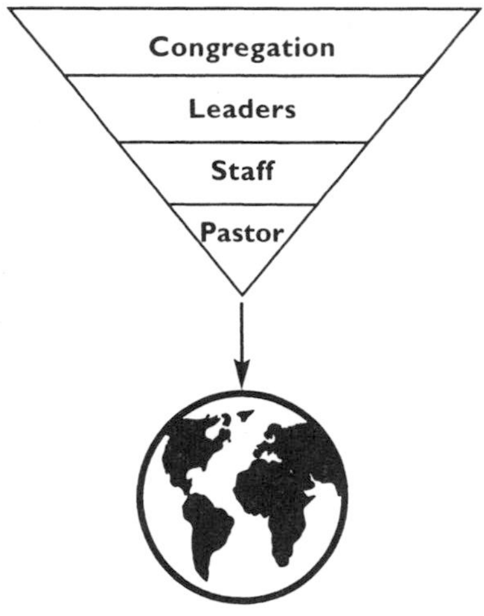

In the first model, the congregation is made up of auditors, observers, supporters—unfulfilled believers. When the commitment narrows and sharpens a bit, the more committed person becomes a leader in the fellowship. As the commitment sharpens more (usually centering *only* in the local body), church staff members emerge. And behold, the most committed person in the church is usually seen to be the pastor! The distortion of this model is evident. So the weight of the body and of its responsibilities rests largely on the pastor. The pastor carries innumerable responsibilities *inside* the body and is often the only one who sees or addresses responsibility *outside* the body. Special programs entice the most committed members to the "special" works of soul-winning, missions, special community services, etc. But the burden of performance, achievement and world impact falls largely upon the pastor.

The results of this model are three-fold:

(1) A very discouraged leadership. Over 1,000 pastors a year are leaving the Southern Baptist preaching ministry. Over 300 a month are being forcibly removed ("fired") from pulpits across the Souther Baptist Convention. Does this embarrass us? It certainly should! And it can be corrected.

(2) A largely "carnal" (self-centered, self-gratifying) church membership. In this model, the members recognize no assignment except church attendance, institutional loyalty, and auditing support. Is it any wonder that they remain carnal?

(3) A largely unevangelized world. Most of the human race have either not heard the Name of Jesus at all, or they have only "barely" heard it. The Christianity of the Book of Acts addressed an even more hopeless situation and completely changed it in a shockingly short time. The situation can be changed just as dramatically today, but not by the continuation of the same crippled model.

The other model is almost the precise opposite of the former one.

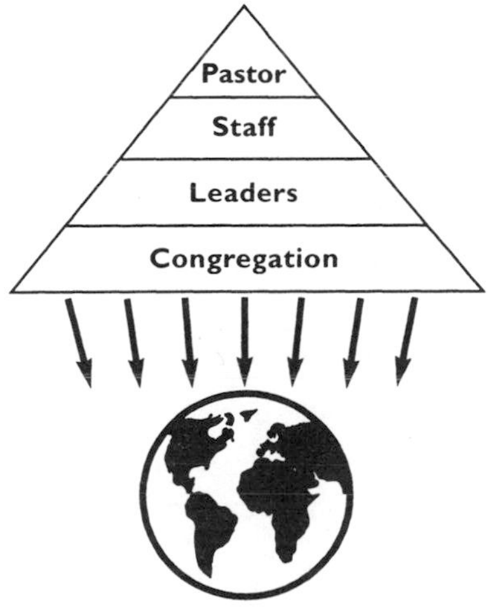

In this model, the pastor has the first responsibility chronologically. His position is one of *responsibility*, not of *prestige*! The responsibility of such a position is immeasurably greater than any prestige that might be gained from it. In fact, it could almost be stated as a rule: any profile of the body that eventuates in the ever-enlarging reputation (for success, ability, etc.) of its leader is highly suspect from a Christian viewpoint! Flesh courts attention, recognition, decoration, and this is only one weakness flesh is heir to! Flesh cannot be trusted with the kind of accolades that are given to super-status, super-star leaders.

The pastor's first responsibility in this model (an American church, thus limited, model) is to equip and infect his staff, and this includes the vision of disciple-making to penetrate the entire world. This common vision should determine the ministry of each staff member, and should dictate his goals for the disciples *he* is building. The pastor is also responsible to equip and infect the leaders, but now he has an incredible advantage. The leaders are now being "doubly equipped" with a common vision and strategy, one directly from the pastor, the other from the staff. And now pastor, staff and leaders will be united in equipping all the saints for their work of ministering. When this expectation is implemented, the "dead weight" will fall away and the "rich young rulers" will be gone. But the *eyes, mouths, ears, hands, knees, and feet* of the body will be seeing, speaking, hearing, doing, kneeling and walking, in complete consolidation—always moving *out* toward the ends of the earth. The local fellowship is not the *primary place* of ministry (though much ministry takes place there), it is the *powerful base* for ministry. The people are automatically showing and sharing Christ *wherever they are,* and they are consciously structuring strategies to personally penetrate to the ends of the earth. At this point, I want to strongly recommend that each reader obtain and master a book by David Bryant entitled, ***In the Gap***. It concerns the vocation of every believer to stand "in the gap" at the *widest* places between the evangelized and the unevangelized in today's world. One of my own men called it "the best book I have ever read outside the Bible."

What is the outcome when the second model becomes a reality? Again, there is a three-fold result:

(1) The most excited and fulfilled leaders on earth.

(2) Ever enlarging numbers of "spiritual" believers (Christ-centered, God-honoring, Spirit-filled, world-impacting saints).

(3) An increasingly evangelized world.

The strategies for implementing the second model are inherent in the Mandate and Model of Jesus and the Mandate and Model of Ephesians 4. But we must be very careful. God's *ultimate* purposes depend on the fulfillment of His *immediate* purposes. Are you yourself being discipled—close-up, "hands-on," with on-the-job assignments for world impact? Are you building into others—close-up, "hands-on," with on-the-job assignments for world impact?

Chapter 9
His Last Words, His Last Will

"But ye shall receive power, after that the Holy Ghost is come upon you: and ye shall be witnesses unto me both in Jerusalem, and in all Judea, and in Samaria, and unto the uttermost part of the earth."

Acts 1:8

George Orwell, the renowned author of ***1984*** and ***Animal Farm***, once wrote, "we have now sunk to a depth at which the restatement of the obvious is the first duty of intelligent men." In today's church, the obvious is revolutionary. Nothing is so poorly obeyed as the "obvious" commission of Jesus. When the obvious is restated and applied, the church is shaken at its foundations.

The commission of Jesus was stated in each of the four Gospels and in the Book of Acts. The Book of Acts is a continuation of the gospel narratives. It is written in chronological sequence and follows an easily discernible geographic pattern, a pattern specified in Acts 1:8: "Jerusalem...Judea... Samaria... the ends of the earth." The Book of Acts may be divided into three segments (1-7, 8-12, 13-28), with the first segment showing how the early church continued in Jerusalem the work that Jesus had begun (Acts 1:1). The second part concerns Gospel progress in Judea and Samaria, and the last part "to the ends of the earth."

Verse eight of Acts one contains the last words that Jesus Christ spoke to His disciples just moments before His ascension to Heaven. The Gospels of Luke and John reveal that the first time Jesus met with His disciples following the resurrection He charged them to be witnesses to all nations. He repeated the charge at least once the same evening. He repeated it again later on the mountain in Galilee as recorded in Matthew 28. And now He is outside the city of Jerusalem, 40 days later, just before His ascension. Thus, the commission should be quite obvious to us. However, one practical question will reveal that we have actually paid it very little attention. *How much of what you do, think, say,* or *make impacts the whole world* ? You see, Jesus was intense about *world involvement,* but *relaxed* about *methods.* We reverse this! We go to one conference after another on methods, but side-step the necessary involvement.

Jesus' command called for action. The Great Commission was never given just to be studied. It is a plan for action. In this study, we will merely examine it again, using Acts 1:8 as our foundation. But, the critical question is: Will you make yourself available at each step for the fulfillment of the Great Commission?

STRATEGY FOR GOSPEL ADVANCE

First, we see in this statement the *Strategy* for Gospel advance. The strategy is contained in the word "witness." This is a cosmopolitan word with an overload of content. The original word is "marturia," which should inform us immediately that this is not a tame word. It is the word from which we get a transliterated English word, the word "martyr." So, the lifestyle pictured in this word is a risk-taking lifestyle. To be a "martyr-witness" is a life-and-death proposition.

Virginia Owens wrote, "Being a Christian is an extreme position, not a safe one. One doesn't follow Christ down the middle of the road toward respectability." One theologian who had begun to appreciate the "extreme position" of Christianity wrote, "Let us collect all the New Testaments there are in existence, let us carry them out to an open place or up on a mountain, and then, while we all kneel down, let someone address God in this fashion: 'Take this Book back again; we men, such as we are now, are no good at dealing with a thing like this, it only makes us unhappy.' My proposal is that like the inhabitants of Gadara, we beseech Christ to 'depart out of our coasts.'" These writers have begun to grasp the radical "martyr-witness" demand of Jesus.

Martyr, this word "martus," occurs over 30 times in the Book of Acts, and is one of the keynotes of the book. It informs us that we are to forget any thought of a "safety-first" lifestyle. Here are some illustrations:

A farmer took his dog hunting in the woods several miles from his house, only to discover that he had forgotten his lunch pail. He put his gun down and told the dog to stay by the gun until he returned. While the farmer was gone, a forest fire swept through the woods and the dog was killed. Later, the farmer found the dog's charred body beside his rifle. He sadly said, "I always had to be careful what I told that dog to do, because he would always do it." Christian friends, Jesus Christ wants us to be so concerned with doing what He says that we forget about the forest fire.

A biology professor expressed a matter-of-fact rule of science in class one day when he said, "Self-preservation is the first law of nature." A Christian student smilingly observed to him after class, "It's most interesting to see the contrast between nature and grace. Self-preservation may be the first law of nature, but self-sacrifice is the first law of grace." He was right!

See the Calvary-sacrifice that is at the very heart of God's grace, and then be reminded that the first principle of Christian discipleship is in these words of Jesus: "If any man will come after Me, let him *deny himself,* and *take up his cross,* and follow Me." To deny myself means that I say to myself what Peter said about Jesus when he denied Him: "I never heard of the man; I do not know the man."

Bruce Morgan wrote, "The trouble with Christians is that nobody wants to kill them anymore." Eugenia Price echoed that thought when she said, "The greatest sin of the church is that it has TAMED Jesus Christ."

The kind of witness which is called for in Acts 1:8 is quite apparently of such a nature that it gets us into constant trouble (but also produces in us constant joy, and is attended by constant miracles).

A meeting of hundreds of religious leaders from across America was held in which the agenda was, "How can we be used to turn this nation back to God?" Each attendant was given opportunity one evening to make a brief response to the question. One black leader arose and said, "Brethren, Christians in America will never again have the desired impact on this society until they lose their fear of dying," and he sat down. Many in the meeting concluded that his may have been the best answer given by anyone present.

Years ago, a great missionary spokesman named Robert Wilder visited tiny Hope College in Michigan to bring a chapel message on world missions. He placed a large map of India in the front of a chapel and installed a metronome before the map. In the message, he declared that every time the metronome clicked, a soul died in India without ever having heard of Christ. That day, Christ and His world vision captured the heart of a young college senior named Samuel Zwemer. As the vision flamed in his heart, he asked God to place him in the hardest spot on earth.

In the course of time, he established residence on the Island of Bahrein in the Persian Gulf, at the very heart of the Islamic world community. This island was often identified in newscasts and newspaper reports of the recent "Gulf War." Zwemer began to print and circulate Gospel tracts, though he hardly had the approval of the Islamic government of the island. In one week, Zwemer's two small daughters, ages four and seven, both died from illness and the oppressive heat. Samuel Zwemer asked the Bahrein officials for permission to bury the bodies of his two precious daughters on the island, but permission was refused on the ground that they were Christians and their bodies would contaminate the soil. Zwemer appealed and permission was granted—if he would dig the graves himself. He did so, and after the burial, he erected a marker which said, "Worthy is the Lamb who was slain to receive riches." This is the heroic, give-all-unto-death lifestyle Jesus called for.

One early missionary society sent 70 missionaries to the nation of Cameroon, the vital "hinge" between west Africa and south and south central Africa. [Incidentally, the Muslims are engaged in a concerted effort today to "capture" Cameroon.] Of the 70, 68 of them died on the field. The average life span of these 70 after arrival on the field was two and one-half years! Many of them actually shipped their coffins with them to the field, knowing that it was unlikely they would return! This is the heroic, give-all-unto-death lifestyle Jesus called for.

A family of missionaries went to China with a "faith missions organization" to proclaim the Gospel there. They went as public school teachers. When they returned, they came back as typical furloughing missionaries—with a box of slides and a visual presentation of their work. "Have slides, will show" seems to be the universal motto of furloughing missionaries. When their presentation and explanation was concluded, a question-and-answer period was allowed. One church member stood and said, "Weren't you afraid you would die over there?" The calculated answer of the husband was, "No, because we DIED BEFORE WE WENT." This echoes the word "martus," or "martyr-witness."

Charles Crowe, Methodist pastor, was driving around the Chicago Loop to his church one morning, as he had done many times before. The church building was renowned as having on its top the tallest steeple of any church building in North America, and on top of it was a large cross. On this particular morning, as Pastor Crowe passed in front of the building he saw a considerable group of people gathered on the sidewalk in front of the building, and they all were looking up. He leaned forward in his car and glanced upward to see what they were gazing at. He turned into the parking lot, parked his car in the "Reserved for Pastor" place, then hurried back around to the front of the building and joined those staring upward.

On top of the cross was a painter with a bucket of paint attached to his suit. He was buckled in place to the cross, and he was slowly painting his way down that metal cross. The cross perceptibly swayed against the sky with every movement he made. The people were watching his delicate and dangerous work. After a few minutes, Charles Crowe left the gathered crowd and started toward his office in the church. Suddenly the Holy Spirit seemed to say, "My child, you have driven that same route hundreds of times and never before was anybody on that sidewalk looking up at the cross. What made the difference today? Simply this: TODAY THE CROSS HAD A MAN ON IT! The world will always stop to see when a true man is really on the cross."

Today the world is saying to the church what Thomas in his doubt and ignorance said about Jesus, "Unless I shall see in His hands the print of the nails, and put my finger into the print of the nails . . . I will not believe." They are looking for the unassuming sacrifice of a Christ-centered Christian, or they will not believe.

It would be well for us to pause a moment and remind ourselves of the only alternative to this Christian lifestyle. Jesus said, "Whosever will save (protect, defend, preserve) his life shall lose it: and whosoever will lose his life for my sake shall find it." The first clause defines the safety-first, me-centered, save-myself-at-all-costs lifestyle. The second clause defines the investing, self-disinterested, other-centered, other-building, Christ-consumed lifestyle—the lifestyle of a Christian.

Two travelers were caught in a heavy blizzard in the far north. As they struggled against the storm, they came upon a man frozen in the snow and thought to be dead. One said, "I have enough to do to keep myself alive; I'm going on." The other said, "I cannot pass a fellow human being while there is the slightest breath left in him." He stooped down and began to warm the frozen man by rubbing him with great vigor. At last the poor man opened his eyes, gradually came back to life and animation, and walked along beside the man who had restored him to life. And what do you think they saw as they struggled along together? They saw the man who took care of his own safety—frozen to death in the snow.

The Good Samaritan had preserved his own life by the vigorous effort required to save the other man. The friction he had produced had aroused the action of his own blood and kept him alive. The rule never fails: "Whosoever (Christian or church) will save his life shall lose it: and whosoever will lose his life for my sake shall find it."

C. S. Lewis captured the adventure of the Christian life in his Chronicles of Narnia series when he had one of the characters in **The Last Battle** *to say, "I'd rather be killed fighting for Narnia than grow old and stupid at home and perhaps go about in a bath chair and then die in the end just the same." Friends, we are going to die one way or another. The Christian commitment is "that Christ may be magnified in my body, whether by life or by death."*

To paraphrase Jesus, "Believer, you are my *evidence*, my *credentials*, my *arguments*, my *recommendations*, my *publicity*, my *advertisements*, my *commercials*." And, the Cross is at the center of any representation of Christ. George Bernard Shaw asked, "Must a Christ be re-crucified in every generation because the world lacks imagination?" The answer to your question, sir, is "Yes," and we are to be the unselfconscious lambs. "You are my martyr-witnesses." This is the strategy for Gospel advance.

SOURCE OF THE GOSPEL WITNESS

Second, we note the *Source* of the Gospel witness. The source of the Gospel witness is seen in the threefold occurrence of the word "you." "Ye shall receive power after the Holy Ghost has come upon you, and ye shall be witnesses unto me." The "you" and "upon you" are plural. The commission is given to the whole Body of Christ and is fulfilled by each member of that Body. You, dear Christian, are involved big-time in the strategy of Jesus. You are the source of the Gospel witness.

Note that the word "you" outnumbers the mention of the Holy Spirit by three to one in this verse. This certainly does not minimize His role; it *maximizes your responsibility.* Who is the "you"? Not angels, nor supermen, nor special people. The text identifies the "you" in the preceding verses. Acts 1:2 specifies them as "the apostles whom Jesus had chosen."

Friends, all the apostles were *men.* This does not minimize the role of women; it maximizes the responsibility of men. The Holy Spirit apparently anticipated the problem of Christian history, that men would tend to easily abdicate their responsibility and turn it over to women. So, today we have mission groups in our churches called "Women's Missionary Society." Thank God for concerned, Godly women; but this is primarily a man's responsibility! You see, if you capture a man, the God-appointed leader in society's basic unit, you stand an excellent chance of capturing everybody in his constituency; but if you capture one of his constituency first (wife, children), you may never capture the leader or any others in his constituency.

Early one cold Good Friday morning some years ago, the People's Church building of downtown St. Paul, Minnesota, caught fire. It was shortly after midnight and the fire department was hindered by the cold in its attempts to put out the fire. By the time they had adjusted, the building had burned to the ground. Early the next morning, church members and townspeople began to gather on the corner where the building was still smoking and the ruins smoldering. The building had been a kind of art museum for religious art, as well as a church building; and, thus, it was a popular spot for tourists.

Right behind the pulpit had stood a replica of "The Appealing Christ," an eight-foot-tall, gleaming white marble statue created by the Danish sculptor, Thorsvalden. As an aside, Stanley Jones, missionary to India, was on a tour of Copenhagen, Denmark, years ago, when the guide brought them to The Church of Our Lady in Copenhagen, where the original of the statue was kept. The statue pictures Jesus standing with face bowed to the ground, hands extended to the world. It is based on Matthew 11:28, "Come unto Me, all ye that labor and are heavy laden, and I will give you rest."

As the group was leaving the church, the guide asked, "Did anyone see the Master's face?" Jones answered, "How could we? It is bowed down to the ground." The guide quietly answered, "That's the point, sir. If you would see the Master's face, you must first kneel at His feet!"

When The People's Church building burned, the statue fell with the floor and caved into the basement below. In the late morning of the following day, several men of the church secured permission to go down into the ruins and see if there were any valuables that survived the fire. They found the statue, streaked and charred, but unharmed except for a large chip out of the square base. They carefully cooled it down, and late that afternoon they picked it up and carried it out of the ruins and onto the street corner. They assigned six men to cordon it off so the passersby and observers would not damage it, then they went back down into the ruins to look again. When they returned to the corner a short time later, the crowd was no longer merely staring down into the ruins of the destroyed building. Instead, they were jockeying for position around the circle, all trying to get a look at the great sculpture.

May I spiritualize the illustration to make a crucial point? You see, Jesus had been in that church all the time, but He had been "chained to the pulpit," and the people on the street had never seen Him. It was only when the church caught fire (!) and the men of the church (!) picked Him up and carried Him out onto the street corner (!) that the "outsiders" saw Him for the very first time! You, Christian believer, are the source of the Gospel witness.

SUBJECT OF THE GOSPEL WITNESS

Then, our verse points out the *Subject* of the Gospel witness. Jesus said, "Ye shall be witnesses UNTO ME." Our witness is not to focus on a church, or a denomination, or a creed, or a doctrine, or a system. It is to focus on Christ. It is our happy privilege to present Him as He presented Himself in His Word, as Redeeming Savior (Acts 1:3), as Risen Lord (1:3), and as Returning King (1:11). What a fathomless Subject! What a captivating theme.

A painting on the wall of a German art gallery illustrates this part of our assignment. The picture shows Martin Luther, the great German reformer, preaching in the high pulpit of a German church. He has a Bible in one hand, is pointing a protruding finger with the other hand, and his mouth is open as if caught in the act of proclamation. He is preaching the Gospel. You see both preacher and audience. But, if you look closely, you observe a peculiarity. No one in the audience is looking at Martin Luther, the preacher! As you follow their gaze, you make a happy discovery. In the corner of the building, there is the dim but unmistakable form of Jesus, the Son of God—and every eye in the place is on Him. They are listening to Luther, but they are looking at Jesus!

This is the desirable outcome of our witness for Christ. We proclaim Him, and He introduces Himself through our witness. So that the attention of the "listener" rests finally on Him.

SCOPE OF THE GOSPEL WITNESS

The text also reveals the *Scope* of the Gospel witness. Note carefully its closing words, "Ye shall be witnesses unto Me BOTH in Jerusalem, AND in all Judea, AND in Samaria, AND unto the uttermost parts of the earth." So,

the *near* people are our assignment— "Jerusalem";
the *neighboring* people are our assignment— "Judea";
the *neglected* people are our assignment— "Samaria" (Samaria represents the people of your worst prejudice); and,
the *next* people are our assignment—"unto the uttermost part of the earth."

"Jerusalem" represents your *immediate situation*, "Judea and Samaria" represent your *intermediate setting*, and the "uttermost part of the earth" represents your *international surroundings*. "Jerusalem" represents our *city* witness, "Judea and Samaria" represent our *country* witness, and the phrase "unto the uttermost part of the earth" represents our *cosmic* witness.

And note carefully that it is not "either/or" with regard to these peoples, it is "both/and." Jesus Christ seriously expects us to take on the whole wide world! How? By learning and following the disciple-making strategy by which we *see the masses through the man*, and *build the man to impact the masses*—the strategy Jesus followed with His Twelve.

The Book of Acts is one of the few books in the Bible that conveniently outlines itself. Chapters one through seven reveal the witness of the early disciples in Jerusalem; chapters 8 through 12, in Judea and Samaria; and chapters 13 through 28, "unto the uttermost parts of the earth."

The real measure of the power and effectiveness of a local body of Christ is: How far does its influence reach? God seriously expects the local church to take on the whole world! After all, Jesus did it with twelve men, and He did it before *telephones, televisions, telethons and telelectronics.* He only had *tell-a-person*! Yet, He impacted the civilized world of that day through His small, rag-tag group of men.

Today, we tend to think that we must win our communities at home before we give the attention He commanded to the world. But that order is reversed. "The light that shines farthest necessarily shines brightest nearest home." Every church should be plotting constantly how it can get the Gospel to as many places in the world as quickly as possible; and its goal should be to build world-visionary disciples who will impact the entire world to the ends of the earth 'til the end of time. God said, "Ask of me, and I will give thee the heathen for thine inheritance, and the uttermost parts of the earth for thy possession" (Psalm 2:8). Then why do we not have the heathen for our inheritance and the uttermost parts of the earth for our possession? The only possible reason is, we are not asking! Quite apparently, the church-at-large does not have on its heart what God has on His heart. What about your church? What about you?

Note, too, that the verse says, "both in Jerusalem and in all Judea, and in Samaria, and unto the uttermost part of the earth." It is not "either/or," it is "both/and." We are to be witnessing in all these places at once, and we are to have them all on our hearts. How? By building a vision for the whole world, and then by building individuals to implement that vision. The scope of our assignment is the whole world.

SECRET OF THE GOSPEL WITNESS

Jesus' words reveal, finally, the *Secret* of the Gospel witness. "Ye shall receive power," He said, "after that the Holy Ghost is come upon you." Note the title, "Holy Ghost." Most Christians prefer the better translation, "Holy Spirit," and for obvious reasons. I like the term, "Holy Ghost," for one reason. We think of a ghost as the part of the person who remains when the body has departed—and that's Who the Holy Spirit is. The best simple way to think of the Holy Spirit is as Jesus without a body. The Holy Spirit is essentially Christ's Replacement in the earth, doing what He did, and carrying on His work.

A little boy said to his mother, "Mama, how does God make it rain?" Then, as an afterthought, he answered his own question: "Oh, never mind, I already know. He gets the Holy Spirit to do it. After all, He does all the work!" The Holy Spirit is the Executive Person in the Godhead. Today, He does all the work!

Then think of the word "power." The Greek word for power is the word "dunamis," and we all know that we derive our English word "dynamite" from that Greek word. However, that association creates a significant problem for us. We associate the word "dynamite" with something highly explosive; and, thus, we tend to expect a highly explosive experience of God's power as representative of Jesus' promise. The problem is two-fold: one, there is no highly explosive experience in the Gospel; and two, the Greeks didn't have dynamite! Dynamite was invented by Alfred Nobel (of Nobel Prize fame) in 1866! To translate the word "dunamis" by our English word "dynamite" is likely to be misleading, causing Christians to seek a "boom" experience instead of allowing the Holy Spirit to produce the efficiency of character and vocation which marked the life and ministry of Jesus.

The power of Acts 1:8 is:
The power of character transformation,
The power of illumination,
The power for communication,
The power for steady action.

It is power *to* witness, as well as power *in* witnessing. Someone defined character power as "the forceful expression of personality," and this is a good definition of God's power. It is the forceful expression of God's personality. It may take the form of a cataclysmic display, but it is far more often expressed as *persuasion* deep within a person's character, and *conviction* that impacts him and others around him. The works of the Holy Spirit promised by Jesus—

Conviction (John 16:7-11),
Illumination (John 16:13-16),
Communication (John 15:26)," and
World impact (Acts 1:8)

—fall far more into the area of dynamic persuasion than the area of demonstrative "boom" experiences.

Note that this power is "received." "Ye shall *receive* power." It is not achieved; it is received. It is not attained; it is obtained. No great talent is required to receive a thing. Both rich men and paupers may receive something that is offered. Presumably, one simply takes it. God is eager to give you the power of the Holy Spirit—but only on His terms and only for His purposes. He has commanded you to be filled with the Holy Spirit, the Person who is God's power.

I John 5:14 says, "This is the confidence that we have in Him, that if we ask anything according to His will, He heareth us."

Since He has commanded us to be filled with the Spirit, we may be confident that this is His will. Thus, we may expectantly ask Him to fill us with His Spirit and simply receive His fullness. Then we may confidently know that the Person of the Holy Spirit is always "traveling with us" as we live to fulfill the Great Commission of our Lord.

Chapter 10
TALLYHO, THE FOX? Oh, Yes, that Title!

Oh, yes, that title! "Tallyho, the Fox!" Occasionally an unaware friend sees it and says, "What does it mean?" I am delighted to finally answer that question, because the entire mandate of Jesus is found in the answer. Here is the background illustration from which this book derived its title:

When dogs run in packs, they will do one or more of four things:

1. They will sleep.
2. They will secure their own survival.
3. They will, if unthreatened, accept new members to the pack.
4. They will fight among themselves.

But there is a "punch line," and it is this:

UNTIL A FOX GOES BY!

What is a "church"? Though the definition is crude, poor, and much oversimplified, a church is Christians running in packs. Theology has been a bit more technical when it calls the church "an assembly or a fellowship of born-again and called-out believers in Jesus Christ banded together for common spiritual purposes." Our definition is simply a picturesque and popularized and illustrative version of the same idea. The biggest fault of the definition lies not in the *analogy*, but in the *verb*. Most churches are not *running*. They are "run" ("he runs this church," "they run this church"; "how is this church run?"), but they are not *running*! They are run like machinery is run, or like a business is run, but they are not running in full pursuit of their assigned goal.

Meanwhile, back to the definition. A church is Christians running in packs. When Christians run in packs (and they do), they will do one or more of four things.

1. They will sleep. The most pertinent Scriptural injunction that could be addressed to many, many churches is, "Awake, you that sleep, and arise from the dead." Many years ago, an evangelical missionary named John Halsy wrote this devastating paragraph:

If I were an author, ambitious of signalizing myself by writing the shortest volume ever known, I would come to some of the members of our genteel suburban churches, and ask their permission to write an account of what they are doing for Christ and for the world. Brief indeed would be the history! A solitary cipher would describe all that many are doing for the Lord that bought them, and for a perishing world! There is a passage that must be a precious solace to some so-called Christians—'We which have believed do enter into rest.' But remember, that is the laborer's rest after toil, not the idler's rest from toil. But I have another passage to set over against this—'Woe unto them that are at ease in Zion!' Yes, woe, for this ease is a guilty thief, rob-

bing believers and churches of their participation with Christ in the most gratifying enterprise on earth.

Neither resurrection nor a wake-up call is too radical in describing the need of many Christians and many churches. I say this with great embarrassment, because I have personally slept through many a trumpet blast from heaven which came to summon me to the front line for a new battle assignment. However, the fact remains that many churches that profess the Name of Christ and avow that they have aligned themselves with the Christianity that produced the Book of Acts are as dead as mausoleums. Heavily chloroformed by the sedative of self, increasingly accustomed to (and naturally desirous of) a Christianity without a cross, eager to popularize Christianity, they (we) seem to be as clueless as "Simple Simon" or "Little Bo Peep" in pursuing the Big Person (one dear Christian brother called it "going hard after Christ") or the Big Purpose (total world impact) or the Big Plan ("making disciples" on Christ's scale and by His strategy). So they sleep.

One wag said, "If all the people who sleep in church were lined up end to end—they'd be more comfortable!"

Another defined preaching as "one man talking in another man's sleep."

One lady called her pastor at 3 a. m. and said, "Pastor, I have a major problem. I have a dreadful case of insomnia, and can't sleep at all. Would you mind preaching to me a little while?"

Fortunately, these are jokes, though an occasional "pew potato in church" makes them justifiable. But when we consider the more tragic reality of Christians somnambulating through life on a self-serving or survival course, and churches vividly and validly described as "sleeping giants" (actually a radical understatement, and sadly underestimated, because most people have no notion of what the giant *should* do or *would* do or *could* do if fully awake and fully active, and thus they have only a mild concept of how asleep the church really is), these assessments are more like judgments than jokes. The church as a "sleeping giant" is clearly Satan's idea.

Now, the second part of the formula:

2. They will secure their own survival. Consider the radical difference between mere survival and true service. The "radical difference" is often not seen because churches usually indulge in a course that is a soothing mixture of the two. They have "services" and offer "opportunities to serve," but does the result come within a million miles of the productivity and outcome of the Book of Acts? True service involves risk, sacrifice, and sheer adventure, and its terms are dictated by the One who manages the enterprise. When someone engages in true service in today's church, he is elevated as an "outstanding Christian," but such categories only publicize the ignorance and indulgence of the "average" believer. Incidentally, is an *average* Christian the worst of the best or the best of the worst? Anyway, the average church is clearly on a survival course, *counting* the sheep more than *feeding* and *equipping* them *to be sent out "as lambs among wolves.* "It is absorbed with buildings, budgets, bulletins, bodies and Bibles—things, which though excellent when used properly, become the "killer bees" when they become ends in themselves. These are (or may be) necessary tangibles in the church, but absorption with them is fatal to the Real Purposes of the church. The church on a survival course is clearly Satan's idea.

Now, the third part of the formula:

3. If unthreatened, the dogs of the pack will accept new members to the pack. Sometimes, the motives for church membership drives, church growth, and "evangelistic crusades" need to be sifted to the very bottom line. Motives are easily distorted and corrupted when they enhance reputations and success stories of individual leaders and the institutions they lead. The very defensiveness and hostility of some leaders is an indication of their hidden awareness of the mixed motives by which they "build" structures, organizations, buildings, crowds, etc. Nobody's motive is perfectly pure, but church growth can conveniently enhance reputations and hide swollen egos while announcing a purity of desire to "serve the Lord." Flesh always lurks as a powerful and deadly potential beneath our all-too-thin layers of spirituality. I am confessing my own weakness at this point, and echoing the common and contrite confession of many honest and godly pastors whom I have known. I know of two fairly small churches which found themselves by location in rapidly growing communities. The reaction of the "old guard" of church leaders to the inevitable church growth was astounding. In each case, the leaders said to the pastor, "We've got to be very careful about all these new people coming, because if it keeps up, we will lose control of our church." (! !) Can such a self-centered, self-serving, survival mentality prevail in a "growing" church? Can such assessments come from church leaders? Every leader with any tenure in the church has encountered such things in church leadership—and possibly in himself. This is only one form that ugly flesh can take. Flesh is usually either performance-oriented or protest-oriented, and spiritual leaders and faithful church members are singled out as prime targets of Satan to provoke such demonstrations of the flesh. After over forty years in the ministry, I find that I must constantly keep the flesh in the "reckoning" position (Romans 6:6, 11; Galatians 2:20).

But remember the punch line of the parable-illustration: ***UNTIL A FOX GOES BY!*** When a fox goes by, and is clearly seen by the dogs, the dogs will hardly have time to sleep. They will not merely secure their own survival anymore. They will accept new members to the "pack" as they come, but the only dogs which will come are those which are willing to get sucked into the vortex of the fox hunt and pursue the fox with all the other dogs on the chase. Though the dogs may bump into each other harder and more frequently than before, they hardly notice the bumps and bruises among themselves—because they have much bigger things to do than growl, bark, and snap at one another. With the fox clearly in view, the dogs will run with a consolidated vision and purpose.

WHAT IS THE FOX?

For the Christian, for the fellowship of believers, *what is The Fox*? I regard it as a "given" that the pursuit point of the Christian life is simply Jesus Christ. The vocation of the Christian life is simply "the pursuit of Jesus," or "following hard after Him." This is final and unarguable with me. But the commanded procedure for enlisting other followers is the one fox that Jesus placed before His disciples as the "Great Commission." Christian leaders tend to create *little foxes* for "their people" to pursue—such things as attendance campaigns, budget drives, building programs, seasonal revivals, and other emphases. But these "little foxes" may "spoil the vines"! They easily become local focal points, funneling the attention of the believers into activities and programs which are far more self-serving than world-impacting.

Several hunters were spending their idle time boasting about their hunting dogs. One said, "I think my dog could pick up a 50-year-old scent on the trail." "Aw, come on," said another, "no dog can pick up a scent that old." "Well, I believe mine can," said the first. A third hunter interrupted and said, "I know how we can find out. I remember my Daddy saying when I was a kid that an old fox used to run every night under our house on the old home place, and that's been forty or more years ago now. Why don't we go out there and see if your dog can pick up the trail?" So they loaded up the dog in the cage in the back of a pick-up and drove out to the old abandoned house. They took the dog to the edge of the house and walked him around one side. Suddenly the dog began yapping and sniffing, yapping and sniffing—and pulling hard at the rope. The owner unfastened the rope and turned the dog loose. The dog darted off across the yard away from the house. When it was about twenty yards from the house, the dog suddenly leaped about six feet in the air! "What's the matter with that crazy dog?" one man cried. "Crazy, nothin'," the former resident replied, "forty years ago there was a fence there, and that fox used to jump through that fence!" The dog continued yapping and sniffing as it ran across the field. Suddenly it veered to the right and pursued a curved course away from the house. The former resident said, "Forty years ago, there was a stand of trees and bushes right there, and the fox used to run around them. Sure 'nuff, that dog of yours is following the exact course of that old fox." The dog kept receding across the field, sniffing and yapping, until he had disappeared. The hunters had been so fascinated watching the dog that they hadn't noticed the dog getting out of sight and sound. Presently one said, "We'd better go after him, and see where he takes us."

But, search as they would, they couldn't find the dog. After hunting for the dog the rest of the day, they had to give up the search, hoping the dog would come back by himself. But their hopes were ill founded. The dog was gone, and they could not find it anywhere. After weeks of waiting and occasional searching and inquiring, they sadly and reluctantly gave up the search for the dog.

Two years later, long after they had given up the search and given up hope, the phone rang in the dog owner's home one night. The caller asked, "Is this the home of Rex, a hunting dog?" "Well, it once was," replied the owner, "but Rex hasn't been seen or heard of here for about two years. Who is this, and what's happening?" "Well, sir, I have a strange situation to report to you. I am the manager of a department store in New York City. I identified your dog by the name and address on his tag. He is downstairs in my store, and I can't get him out. He has an old fox stole cornered in the basement, and we can't get him to leave it!" The owner quickly recovered from his astonishment, sized up the situation, and said, "Sir, would you consider shipping my dog back home at my expense?" "I've thought of that, and already checked it out," came the reply, "and the cost of shipping the dog is very expensive." "Well, how much is the fox stole?" the dog owner asked. "Only $65," replied the store manager. After a pause, the dog owner slowly asked, "Then, sir, would you ship the fox stole to me today, then leave the basement door of your store open for five minutes tomorrow?"

Friends, *it is time*—for God's sake, for Christ's sake, for the sake of multitudes of lost souls, for the sake of the fellowship of believers, for the sake of all that is true and noble and good, that we go back to our spiritual "home place," pick up an old scent (the Great Commission), a scent which will prove to be more gratifying than the Red Herrings of the world and the flesh, and get on The Trail of The Big Fox.

What is The Big Fox? The Big Fox is *total world impact. Total. Total World. Total World Impact.* Total impact of the total world. This is Christ's Big Fox—which He commanded His people to "chase." *Every Christian should take a long, absorbing look at The Big Fox every day of his life.* A long, absorbing look at The Fox will entail the understanding of several key concepts. One is ***vision.*** Another is ***strategy.*** Another is ***motivated and motivational multiplication***, a concept which apparently played a major role in the production of the Book of Acts. And the last concept is ***the understanding of Total World Impact***—the goal to impact the total world, and the goal of an impact that is "total," that is, inclusive of all the mandated and revealed means to accomplish the task.[1]

---

[1]Nothing said in this brief chapter is to be taken as anti-church in any way. There is already far too much wholesale "church-bashing" for me to be guilty of adding more. I hope this caution is taken with grave seriousness. God's glorious church—the Body and Bride of Christ, the Building of God, "the pillar and ground of the truth," needs enlarging numbers of praying, going, giving, supporting adherents like it has never needed them before. But a counterfeit purpose or procedure ("little foxes") will destroy the glory of the church and allow it to be justly criticized and rejected by many. May Christ's Body give Him a fully functional organism for fulfilling the Great Commission! May Christ's Bride be so in love with Him that the mere mention of the Great Commission is to be constrained by the love of Christ to fulfill it! May the Building of God be such a Temple that it will exhibit our God to the whole wide world!

Conclusion
A Wild Dog's Life

The men with whom I have been privileged to work in the disciple-making, world-impacting process are some of the most motivated Christians I have ever known. A worthy example is a young disciple named Ian Bowers. Ian has been growing in disciple-making discernment and involvement for several years. Sometime ago, he wrote a poem about the "Tally Ho, the Fox" illustration. I have read it quite a number of times. I wept when the message of the poem really came home to my heart. With Ian's permission, I conclude this volume with his poem. I pray that you will be blessed as I was.

A wild dog's life is simple,
Though not a life of ease
A new perspective I will give
We live a life of need.

These needs seem to control us
And dominate our lives
But every day I wonder if
Those needs are but a lie.

You see each day is ours to conquer
No schedule do we keep
But then this need, it comes upon us
It is the need to ***sleep****.*

In a field or 'neath a shade tree
Or under a starry sky
You long for the dog's life
As you see us lying by.

But turn not from my story now
Listen, and listen well
And find that a sleeping dog's life
Is but a step from Hell.

For in a moment awakened
Something moves inside me
And I am hungry, O so hungry
It is the need to ***eat****.*

In town I'd find some garbage scraps
In the woods a little beast
But once I had been satisfied
I quickly returned to sleep.

And by this I was not threatened
I counted it a treasure gold
When ***a dog who was lazier than me***
Was welcomed in the fold*.*

Is it still the dog's life
Your heart is yearning for?
You do not have a clue my friend
For there is much, much more.

My story soon will be quite clear
For now receive this light
The dark side of a wild dog's life
It is the need to ***fight****.*

But fight for what? I'll ask you now
Can you tell me the time
To rise against my fellow dog
Or maybe take his life?

He is a dog with fur and tail
And teeth and eyes to see
Yet he must prove he's better
Or sometimes it is me.

So snarl and growl, bark and bite
Our pride to satisfy
One will win this foolish fight
And one might even die.

And when the fight is over
Always loss, there is not gain
All that we have really proved
Is that dogs can be quite vain.

The need to fight, I do not think
Is how it should be said,
Instead I think that we are bored
And but a step from dead.

Are you listening carefully?
Are you listening, my friend?
My story is not over
For now it just begins.

There is one need that I admit
I say with no disgrace
This wild dog loves, yea even lives
To enter in the chase.

But not just any chase, my friend
A chase that's grand, divine
A chase that challenges my life
And captivates my mind.

No, not the little foxes
I've chased them all before
But they are quickly caught, consumed
And I was quickly bored.

Then one day it happened,
I never will forget
Something rolling through the air
My appetite it whet.

I raised my nose up to the sky
I rose up to my feet
And then I saw the other dogs
Just as alert as me.

Salvador was the leader
Of our motley twelve dog pack
His fur was golden yellow
With red stripes down His back.

This is the one you've waited for
He said with a gleam in His eye
This is the fox that if you would catch
Will surely cost your life.

Raise your noses into the air
Breathe that scent, that smell
Learn it, learn it, learn it
Learn it, learn it well.

And when you cannot see me
Raise your noses into the air
Pick up the scent and follow
And know that I am there.

I felt my heart increase its beat
My pulse began to swell
As stronger, ever stronger
Came that scent, that smell.

And then without a warning
Like a fiery bolt of light
Our leader turned and launched Himself
Into the dark of night.

We stood for but a moment
And looked in each other's eyes
We knew just what the cost would be
But only guessed as to the prize.

And if we were to catch this fox,
We could no longer delay
For the task became much larger
As the scent began to fade.

It must stay fresh upon our nose
Our purpose must be clear
We will catch this mighty fox
TALLY HO!!! will be our cheer.

My nostrils flared, my muscles tensed
I leapt from out my place
My paws did pound upon the ground
And thus began the chase.

But do not think you know my friend
What I was racing for
The prize was not found in the fox
The prize was something more.

No longer driven by a need
To sleep or even eat
Instead I was in full control
Of that which once held me.

Are you listening closely?
Are you listening, my friend?
The prize is this: A life well-lived
With a purpose to its end.

I'd stop to eat, I'd stop to sleep
Exhaustion told me when
But once my strength had been renewed
The chase was on again.

And as for fighting, learn this truth
We did not have the time!
We'd found the challenge of our life
To captivate our mind.

For we did not chase blindly
A fox we could not see
We knew he was a shrewd one
So we ran with a strategy.

We did not judge nor threaten
Newcomers to the pack
We boldly shared our vision
And set them on his track.

This track, this trail, the grandest prize
Some dogs just would not see
Still others entered in the chase
It would not die with me.

Now learn this old dog's lesson
Learn it, learn it well
For each dog fallen by the side
Let three more join the swell.

Ensure the chain is not broken
Ensure the chase will go on
Invest yourself in some wild dog's life
And show him the race to run.

So do not think you see me now
A feeble dog near death
My light will shine still brightly
When I've offered my last breath.

For I've taught other wild dogs
This I taught them well
I taught them how to raise their noses
I taught them how to smell.

Another thing I taught them
The most important one
I taught them all a strategy I lived and taught "The Run."

Now you have heard my story
Did you listen well?
Are you longing for the dog's life
That's but a step from Hell?

The challenge is before you
Will you multiply the swell?
Go and enter in the chase
Run it AND RUN IT WELL!!

— *Ian Bowers*

APPENDIX

Chapter Outlines

Chapter 1 How Vital is Vision? (Proverbs 29:18)

I. A Spiritual Concept
   A. The Importance of Vision
   B. The Interpretation of Vision
II. A Sad Condition
   A. No Vision in the Pulpit
   B. No Vision in the Pew
   C. No Vision in Public Life
III. The Serious Consequences
   A. The People Cast Off Restraint - the moral consequences of no vision
   B. The People Disintegrate - the social consequence of no vision
   C. The People are Exposed to Judgment - the personal consequences of no vision
   D. The People Perish - the spiritual, eternal consequences of no vision

Chapter 2 The Commission That Determines Our Mandate (Matthew 28:18-20)

I. The Assurance Behind the Commission

A. Divine Authority

B. Delegated Authority

C. Deserved Authority

D. Defined Authority

II. The Assignment Within the Commission

A. The Church's (Christian's) Only Marching Orders

B. Division of the Commission into Parts

1. Employ the Personnel
2. Enter the Field
3. Enlarge the Vision
4. Evangelize the Prospects
5. Enlist the Evangelized
6. Educate and Edify the Enlisted
7. Expect Him to Work

C. The Great Commission or the Great Omission?

Chapter 3 The Concept That Determines Our Method (Matthew 28:19)

I. Disciple-Making

A. Disciple

B. Discipler

C. Discipling

D. Disciplines

II. Disciple-Making That Produces a Ministry of Multiplication

Chapter 4 The Key That Hangs on the Front Door of Church History (Acts 1:1-5)

I. Previous Document Mentioned
  A. The Gospel According to Luke
  B. Who Was Luke and How Did He Get Into The Story?
  C. Devotional Truths
    1. The Analogy of the Church as "The Body of Christ"
    2. Luke Wrote Two Incredible Documents
II. Personal Disciple Identified
  A. One-Fourth of the New Testament was written by One Person!
  B. Why Did Luke Write These Two Documents to One Person?
  C. Personal Testimony
III. Plain Declaration of Purpose for Writing
  A. All That Jesus Began Both to Do and to Teach
  B. What is Jesus Doing Now?
    1. He is Continuing to Do and Teach
    2. Each Believer is a Living Container of His Personal Presence
  C. What Kind of Persons Did Jesus Use?
    1. Common Men

2. Chosen Men
3. Convinced Men
4. Commanded Men
5. Controlled Men

Chapter 5 Essentials for Making Disciples, or
The Doctor's Cure for the Great Omission
(Luke 1:1-14)

I. Personal Responsibility
II. Painstaking Research
III. Precise Resources
IV. Persistent Reproduction

Chapter 6 God's Multiplication Table (2 Timothy 2:2)

I. The Profile of a Multiplying Disciple
   A. A Son
   B. A Soldier
   C. An Athlete
   D. A Husbandman
   E. A Workman
   F. A Vessel
   G. A Servant
II. The Procedure for Multiplying Disciples
   A. How Does the Process Reach a Disciple?
   B. What Does the Process of Hearing Entail?
   C. Once a Disciple is Equipped, What Does He Do?
III. Illustrations that Show the Importance & Potential

of Multiplication

A. An Evangelist

B. A Daily Day of Pentecost

C. Doubling of Pennies

D. The Vision of World Impact by Disciple-Making

Chapter 7 The Genius of Jesus' Strategy (I Thess. 3:8)

Chapter 8 How This Standard Works in a Church (Ephesians 4:7-14)

I. The Giver of the Gifts

A. He Descended

B. He Ascended

C. He Transcends

II. The Gifts Themselves

A. Apostles

B. Prophets

C. Evangelists

D. Pastor-Teachers

III. The Goals for the Giving of These Gifts

A. To Enlist Members

B. To Equip the Members

C. To Employ the Members

Chapter 9 His Last Words, His Last Will (Acts 1:8)

I. Strategy for Gospel Advance

II. Source of the Gospel Witness

III. Subject of the Gospel Witness

IV. Scope of the Gospel Witness

- A. Your Immediate Situation
- B. Your Intermediate Setting
- C. Your International Surroundings

V. Secret of the Gospel Witness

Recommended Reading List

DISCIPLE-MAKING

Adsit, Christopher B., *Personal Disciplemaking*

*Coleman, Robert E., *The Master Plan of Evangelism*

Coleman, Robert E., *The Master Plan of Discipleship*

Coleman, Robert E., *The Great Commission Lifestyle*

Davis, Ron Lee, *Mentoring: The Strategy of the Master*

*Eims, Leroy, *The Lost Art of Disciple Making*

Foster, Robert, *The Navigator*

Fryling, Alice, *Disciplemakers' Handbook*

Hadidian, Allan, *Successful Discipling*

*Henrichsen, Walter, *Disciples Are Made Not Born*

Hull, Bill, *Jesus Christ Disciplemaker*

Hull, Bill, *The Disciple Making Church*

Hull, Bill, *The Disciple Making Pastor*

Jones, Milton, *Discipling: The Multiplying Ministry*

Kuhne, Gary, *The Dynamics of Discipleship Training*

Moore, Waylon, *Multiplying Disciples*

Moore, Waylon, *New Testament Follow-Up*

Peterson, William, *The Discipling of Timothy*

*Skinner, Betty, *Daws*

Staton, Knofel, *Check Your Discipleship*

Trotman, Dawson, *Born to Reproduce* (booklet)

RELATIONAL LIVING

Erwin, Gayle, *The Jesus Style*

George, Bob, *Classic Christianity*

George, Bob, *Growing in Grace*

Johnston, Jon, *Walls or Bridges*

Kidd, Sue Monk, *God's Joyous Surprises*

*Larson, Bruce, *No Longer Strangers*

Larson, Bruce, *Setting Men Free*

Maxwell, John, *Be a People Person*

McGinnis, Alan Loy, *Bringing Out the Best in People*

McGinnis, Alan Loy, *The Friendship Factor*

WORLD MISSIONS

Berry, Harold, *Islam* (a booklet from Back to the Bible)

Borthwick, Paul, *A Mind for Missions*

Borthwick, Paul, *How to Be a World Class Christian*

*Bryant, David, *In the Gap*

Howard, David, *The Great Commission for Today*

Johnstone, Patrick, *Operation World*

Kyle John, *The Unfinished Task*

Kyle, John, *Finishing the Task*

Otis, George, Jr., *The Last of the Giants*

Shibley, David & Naomi, *The Smoke of a Thouand Villages*

Sjogren, Bob, *Run With the Vision*

Stearns, Bill & Amy, *Catch the Vision 2000*

Taylor, Dr. and Mrs Howard J., *Hudson Taylor, God's Man in China*

Tucker, Ruth, *From Jerusalem to Irian Jaya*

Winter, Ralph, *Perspectives On the World Christian Movement*

Yamamori, Testsunao, *God's New Envoys*

Yohannan, K. P., *The Coming Revolution in World Missions*

Yohannan, K. P., *Why the World Waits*

FOR CURRICULUM STUDY

*Blanchard, John, *Will the Real Jesus Please Stand Up?*

Bridges, Jerry, *The Discipline of Grace*

Bunyan, John, *Pilgrim's Progress* (do not read this without gathering illustrations by topic)

Horne, Charles, *The Doctrine of Salvation*

Hubbard, David Allen, *What's God Been Doing All This Time?*

Kennedy, James, *Knowing the Whole Truth*

*Lindsey, Hal, *The Liberation of Planet Earth* (a good study of basic Gospel words & doctrines)

Lockyer, Herbert, *All the Doctrines of the Bible*

McCallum, Dennis, *Christianity: the Faith that Makes Sense*

Shaw, Mark, *Doing Theology With Huck and Jim*

Watson, David, *Is Anyone There?*

Watson, David, *My God is Real*

Wiersbe, Warren, *Key Words of the Christian Life*

FOR BIBLE STUDY

Genesis:

Griffith-Thomas, W. H., *Genesis*

Phillips, John, *Exploring Genesis*

Exodus:

Meyer, F. W., *Exodus–Volumes I & II*

Pink, A. W., *Gleanings in Exodus*

Leviticus:

Bonar, A., A., *An Exposition of Leviticus*

Seiss, J. A., *The Gospel in Leviticus*

Numbers:

Deuteronomy:

Joshua:

Pink, A. W., *Gleanings in Joshua*

Meyer, F. B., *Joshua*

Judges:

Hunter, John, *Judges and a Permissive Society*

Ruth:

Wiersbe, Warren, *Put Your Life Together*

DeHaan, M. R., *The Romance of Redemption*

I & II Samuel:

Pink, A. W., *The Life of David*

Redpath, Alan, *The Making of a Man of God*

I & II Kings:

Meyer, F. W., *Elijah*

Rendall, T. S., *Living the Abundant Life*

I & II Chronicles:

Ezra:

Nehemiah:

Redpath, Alan, *Victorious Christian Service*

Esther:

Stedman, Ray, *The Queen and I*

Thomas, Ian, *If I Perish… I Perish*

Job:

Psalms:

Phillips, John, 3 volumes, *Exploring the Psalms*

Spurgeon, Charles, *The Treasury of David*

Proverbs:

Ecclesiastes:

Stedman, Ray, *Solomon's Secret*

Swindoll, Charles, *Living on the Ragged Edge*

Song of Solomon:

Phillips ,John, *Exploring the Song of Solomon*

Burrowes, George, *The Song of Solomon*

Isaiah:

Young, E. J., *The Book of Isaiah*

Youngblood, Ronald, *Themes From Isaiah*

Jeremiah:

Peterson, William, *The Prophet Who Wouldn't Quit*

Morgan, G. Campbell, *Studies in the Prophecy of Jeremiah*

Ezekiel:

Daniel:

Campbell, Donald, *Daniel: Decoder of Dreams*

Hosea:

Morgan, G. Campbell, *The Heart & Holiness of God*

Riggs, Jack, *Hosea's Heartbreak*

Joel:

Price, Walter, *The Prophet Joel*

Amos:

Honeycutt, Roy, *Amos & His Message*

Obadiah:

Jonah:

Ferguson, Sinclair, *Man Overboard*

Weiss, G. Christian, *Wrong-Way Jonah*

Micah:

Nahum:

Habbakkuk:

Lloyd-Jones, D. Martyn, *From Fear to Faith*

Zephaniah:

Haggai:

Zechariah:

Baron, David, *The Visions & Prophecies of Zechariah*

Malachi:

Kaiser, Walter, *God's Unchanging Love*

Morgan, G. Campbell, *Malachi's Message For Today*

Matthew:

Morgan, G. Campbell, *Gospel According to Matthew*

Wiersbe,Warren, *Meet Your King*

Mark:

Scroggie,Graham, *Gospel of Mark*

Stedman, Ray, 2 volumes, *The Servant Who Rules; The Ruler Who Serves*

Luke:

Blanchard, John, *Look Through Luke*

Morgan, G. Campbell, *Gospel According to Luke*

John:

Hendriksen,William, *Gospel of John*

Powell, Ivor, *John's Wonderful Gospel*

Acts:

Stedman, Ray, 2 volumes, *Birth of the Body; Growth of the Body*

Morgan, G. Campbell, *Acts of the Apostles*

Romans:

Phillips, John, *Exploring Romans*

Wiersbe, Warren, *Be Right*

I Corinthians:

Blair, Allen, *Living Wisely*

Stedman, Ray, *Expository Studies in I Corinthians*

II Corinthians:

Redpath, Alan, *Blessings Out of Buffetings*

Wiersbe,Warren, *Be Encouraged*

Galatians:

Gromacki, Robert, *Stand Fast in Liberty*

Stott, John R. W., *The Message of Galatians*

Ephesians:

Anders, Max, *The Good Life*

Paxson, Ruth, *The Wealth, Walk & Warfare of the Christian*

Philippians:

King, Guy, *Joy Way*

Meyer, F. B., *Epistle to the Philippians*

Colossians:

King, Guy, *Crossing the Border*

Wiersbe, Warren, *Be Complete*

I & II Thessalonians:

Hiebert, Edmund, *The Thessalonian Epistles*

Wiersbe, Warren, *Be Ready*

I Timothy:

Gromacki, Robert, *Stand True to the Charge*

King, Guy, *A Leader Led*

II Timothy:

King,Guy, *To My Son*

Stott, John R. W., *Guard the Gospel*

Titus:

Getz, Gene, *A Profile for a Christian Lifestyle*

Patterson, Paige, *Living in the Hope of Eternal Life*

Hebrews:

Henrichsen, Walter, *After the Sacrifice*

Phillips, John, *Exploring Hebrews*

James:

Blanchard, John, *Truth for Life*

King, Guy, *A Belief That Behaves*

I Peter:

Hiebert, Edmond, *First Peter*

Wiersbe, Warren, *Be Hopeful*

II Peter:

I John:

King, Guy, *The Fellowship*

Wiersbe, Warren, *Be Real*

Revelation:

Coleman, Robert, *Songs of Heaven*

Phillips, John, *Exploring Revelation*

FOR BACKGROUND STUDY

*Baxter, J. Sidlow, *Explore the Book*

Henry, Matthew, *Commentary on the Whole Bible*

*Mears, Henrietta, *What the Bible is All About*

Phillips, John, *Exploring the Scriptures*

Questions & Suggestions For Study of This Book

For chapter one, "How Vital Is Vision?'

1. Give two definitions of Divine vision.

2. What are the consequences that follow when God's people have no vision?

For chapter two, "The Commission that Determines Our Mandate."

1. What are the seven assignments of the Great Commission? How many are commands?

2. What alternate plan has Satan offered under each of the seven assignments?

For chapter three, "The Concept that Determines Our Method."

1. Give definitions of each of these words: "Disciple," "Discipler," "Discipling," and "Disciplines."

2. What is the difference between typical church-going Christianity and a Christian life that produces a ministry of multiplication?

For chapter four, "The Key that Hangs at the Front Door of Church History."

1. Give a brief summary of the Paul-to-Luke-to-Theophilus discipling process.

2. What evidence do we have that Theophilus "caught" the strategy and "ran with it"?

For chapter five, "The Essentials of Making Disciples, or The Doctor's Cure for the Great Omission."

1. List and summarize the four things that Dr. Luke did to disciple Theophilus.

2. How vital is each step in the total process? Can a disciple-maker omit even one of these and hope for success in building a disciple? How many of these steps are you presently engaging in for the sake of a disciple?

For chapter six, "God's Multiplication Table."

1. What are the seven profile pictures of a disciple in II Timothy 2? Is this an exhaustive picture, or merely suggestive?

2. Explain the generational strategy of II Timothy 2:2, showing what is necessary to "guarantee" at least four generations of multiplication.

For chapter seven, "The Genius of Jesus' Strategy."

1. Explain the organizational genius of Jesus' strategy as He trained His twelve Apostles.

2. Do you believe the chart in this chapter to be coincidental, incidental or fundamental to Jesus' strategy?

For chapter eight, "How This Standard Works in a Church"

1. Can the strategy of multi-generational disciple-making work in an institutional church? How?

2. Draw the contrasting charts shown in this chapter, showing the traditional model and then the model suggested by Ephesians 4:7-14.

For chapter nine, "His Last Words, His Last Will"

1. What one word in the Book of Acts reveals God's strategy for Gospel advance? What are the two meanings of this word? What is the relation between the two meanings of this word?

2. Who constitutes God's "labor force," and in what fields are the laborers to work?

3. By what means are the laborers to accomplish this assignment?

For chapter ten, "Tally Ho, the Fox? Oh, Yes, That Title!"

1. Explain the "Fox" analogy.

2. Is this analogy true to what you have observed in the local church?

3. What is the "Big Fox"?